Living with Paradox

By the same author

Blunt (Bishop A. W. F. Blunt of Bradford)
(Mountain Press 1969)

Ambrose Reeves
(Gollancz 1973)

Cornish Bishop (Bishop J. W. Hunkin of Truro)
with Alan Dunstan
(Epworth Press 1977)

Eric Treacy
(Ian Allan 1980)

Defender of the Church of England (Bishop R. R. Williams of Leicester)
(Amate Press 1984)

Wand of London (Bishop J. W. C. Wand)
(Mowbray 1987)

Joost de Blank: Scourge of Apartheid
(Muller, Blond and White 1987)

Living with Paradox

John Habgood, Archbishop of York

JOHN S. PEART-BINNS

Darton, Longman and Todd
London

First published in 1987 by
Darton, Longman and Todd Ltd
89 Lillie Road, London SW6 1UD

ISBN 0 232 51662 6

British Library Cataloguing in Publication Data

Peart-Binns, John S.
Living with paradox: John Habgood, Archbishop of York.
1. Habgood, John 2. Church of England—Bishops—Biography
I. Title
283′.092′4 BX5199.H1/

ISBN 0-232-51662-6

Phototypeset by Input Typesetting Ltd, London SW19 8DR
Printed and bound in Great Britain by
Anchor Brendon Ltd, Tiptree, Essex

for
ANNIS
with love

Contents

Acknowledgements

Let the first be last!

The nature of the work – study, not biography – demands intensive scrutiny rather than extensive contacts. However, some personal exposure is necessary. A number of people generously responded to my request for help in perceiving, pursuing and penetrating the many themes and areas of interest, concern and conviction of John Habgood. In all kinds of ways they have enabled me to get a sense of perspective about the subjects under scrutiny, including the subject himself!

First, my grateful thanks to those who responded by letter or in conversation, including the Archbishop of Canterbury (Robert Runcie), Bishops Michael Ball CGA (Jarrow), Allen Goodings (Quebec), Alec Hamilton (formerly Jarrow), Colin James (Winchester), David Jenkins (Durham), Edward F. B. Moore (formerly Kilmore), Bruce Rosier (Willochra), W. B. Spofford (formerly Eastern Oregon) and John S. Spong (Newark); Lords Adrian, Blanch (formerly Archbishop of York) and Wrenbury; the late Professor Sir Bryan Matthews; Eric Heaton (Dean of Christ Church, Oxford), J. G. E. Marchant (formerly Archdeacon of Auckland), Michael Perry (Archdeacon of Durham); Professors D. C. Spanner and L. G. Whitby; Doctors Paul Abrecht, Oliver Barclay and Robert E. D. Clark; the Reverends Peter A. Baldwin, Roger Clarke, Geoffrey Kemp and Nicolas Stacey; Major W. F. Batt; Messrs Stephen Lloyd, Derek Pattinson and Patrick Wilkinson; Mrs Pamela Garman (the Archbishop's sister); Mrs Barbara Weeks; and Miss Edith Barnes. To each of them I say 'thank you'.

Secondly, I place on record my indebtedness to Bishop

Kenneth Woollcombe for his assistance and for reading the completed manuscript and offering observations on it.

Thirdly, there are the people of my own home who have been patient when they have seen me walking along the canal towpath from the station laden with papers and sermons galore, all to be outwardly read and inwardly digested. In that way John Habgood has been our 'temporary-permanent' resident over a long period. Now there is a gap. The dedication is elsewhere but this is the place to say thank you to my family and for their love which alone makes everything worthwhile.

Now, the first shall be last!

Once the proposal of this study was approved John Habgood not only let me enter his mind but also welcomed me into his home. It has been a contrast and joy to move from study to 'home' at Bishopthorpe, grappling with ideas in the one and relaxing and laughing with the family in the other. Special thanks go to Mrs Rosalie Habgood for her assistance, warm welcome and hospitality.

My biggest debt of gratitude is to John Habgood himself for agreeing to co-operate with this study. It carries no *imprimatur*, for that would be against the nature of the book and the spirit of the man! The Archbishop has been as generous with the time he has put at my disposal as with the material he has let me see and have on loan. He has responded to my probings and in turn has illuminated and swept some dusty corners of my ignorance. I think we have both enjoyed the encounter. He has read the manuscript and offered his observations. Some corrections and a few adjustments have been made. But the selection and treatment are my own.

The archiepiscopate is young. The life and work continue. I hope this study, necessarily partial and tentative, will be of interest and use to those in church and society who want to know more about the manner and mind of the man who is the Primate of England: John Stapylton Habgood, Archbishop of York.

JOHN S. PEART-BINNS
Hebden Bridge
November 1986

Apologia

When John Stapylton Habgood was placed in the throne at York Minster on 18 November 1983, the Dean of York (Ronald Jasper) prayed that God would make the new archbishop 'humble, just and true'. There was something unexpected about the choice of words and 'unexpectedness' is a strong ingredient in John Habgood's life and thought.

Under his leadership the Church cannot be a ready reckoner where stereotyped answers are given to intractable problems or glib pronouncements made on complex issues. National initiatives, blueprints and revivalist campaigns are unlikely to emanate from Bishopthorpe, York. Yet these are the kinds of semi-vacuous activities which people mistakenly regard as signs of strong leadership.

Habgood's rationale of leadership is theological, interpreted in an unusual way. He has described the essence of the theological approach as being 'the unfamiliar angle, the unexpected shaft of light, the revealing silence which conveys more than could have been said in words'. There are words, an abundance of them, but they are unmistakably his own. The imprecision of language, with slogans standing for thought (the Church is as bad as anyone) is anathema to him. It is natural for him to handle deep religious themes without the usual conventional language. This makes issues come alive, take on significance, point somewhere, instead of being destroyed by jargon.

In an age when stridency and confrontation are predominating tendencies, words such as 'compromise' and 'reconciliation' are regarded as the paper weapons of a weak, defeatist and ineffectual army. Reconciliation is important to Habgood. Contrary to the laws of physics, the greater the friction between people, the colder they become. The reconciler draws the sting of friction into himself. It is not a comfortable position. Habgood says: 'The reconciler must do more than say reconciling words. It is frequently claimed, as an excuse for causing suffering, that in a battle somebody must get hurt. The reconciler accepts that the person who suffers may be himself.'

Habgood once described himself as a 'passionate moderate'. This is Christian strength, not, as the world may term it, a weakness. He wrote:

> To live with opposites, not in weak compromise, but constantly allowing different convictions, different emphases, different insights to react fruitfully on each other, entails a kind of death. We have to let others be themselves. If need be, we have to let them wound us. We have to reject utterly the sort of touchiness and pettiness and narrow-mindedness which can so quickly make us all scurry away from one another behind our defences. We have to bear the pain of difference if we are to know the joy of discovery.

The reconciler and passionate moderate is also a radical thinker, another word which is suspect. It is too often assumed that radical thinkers, in any sphere of thought, have few if any dogmatic convictions. Habgood agrees with Dorothy L. Sayers who wrote: 'Dogma, far from being an arrogant and uncritical assertion of knowledge, can be a protection against superficial explanations, a stimulus to look deeper.' Habgood has not only released depth charges into the quiescent waters of the Church but also continually keeps his own critical (though not necessarily self-critical) faculty alive by never withdrawing his attentive antennae from the world of today.

The root of all real intelligence is scepticism. Habgood shares something with T. S. Eliot who said: 'My own beliefs are held with a scepticism which I never even hope to be quite rid of.' He would go further with Eliot, who wrote of Pascal: 'For every man who thinks and lives by thought must have his own scepticism, that which stops at the question, that which ends in denial, or that which leads to faith and which is somehow integrated into the faith which transcends it. And Pascal, as the type of one kind of religious believer who is highly passionate and ardent, but passionate only through a powerful and regulated intellect is, in the first sections of his unfinished Apology for Christianity, facing unflinchingly the demon of doubt which is inseparable from the spirit of belief.' In retrospect it seems that when Habgood had a sudden evangelical conversion, he held back from total surrender and maintained his scepticism and his intellectual self-respect.

Habgood's own thinking does not take place in the sanctified calm of the Athenaeum but in his study, while travelling and in small groups where hard and precise thinking – not waffle – is the strong meat available. These groups are on the exciting frontiers of many disciplines: launching-pads not resting-places.

My aim in this book is to study and share with my readers the thought of John Habgood, by reference to his published and unpublished writings. With the additional benefit of personal conversations this means estimating quality, not faultfinding. I will endeavour to illuminate what I describe. The context of many words and a few actions will be clearly described. Sometimes I will serve my offering neat. I will not read into his words or works, thoughts or actions, meanings which were never there or give them an inflated significance. The nuances, paradoxes and ambiguities will disclose themselves. Writing in 1843 in *Either/Or*, Kierkegaard (who much interests Habgood) referred to the confusion of *his* age: 'We look for a thing where we ought not to look for it, and what is worse, we find it where we ought not to find it; we wish to be edified in the theatre, aesthetically impressed in church, we would be converted by novels, get enjoyment out of books of devotion, we want philosophy in the pulpit, and the preacher in the professorial chair.'

An Apologia is more than an explanation. It is a vindication. This book is being written because I consider Habgood's writings are worth studying and pursuing. To many people he is the quintessential Anglican – reasonable, morally sensitive, cool, non-dogmatic, non-sectarian. He is the more valuable because such men are in perilously short supply. Whether we are meandering or pushing our way towards the next century it is a bracing tonic to share the journey with someone who is thinking his way through the moral, social, economic, political and theological turbulence which is both apparent and real. I think you will find some of Habgood's words enlightening, some irritating, some bewildering, some full of paradox but most of them thought-provoking and worth lingering over, and a few may cause you to consider changing direction.

One of the interesting aspects of some of Habgood's writing is that he conveys the feeling of being a scientist as well as a Christian. His thinking starts with God and he tackles the biggest questions. Is God a question or an answer? Why value human beings? Who am I? Where do we come from? Where are we going? What is life for? There may be nothing new about the questions, but some of the answers will be new. Again the word that comes to mind is 'unexpected'.

First God, then the world. Habgood is an internationalist, even universalist. And the natural world is his dwelling-place. An unashamed idealist, he responds to such words as 'aspiration', 'hope', 'longing', 'vision'.

After God and the world there is the Church. A leader writer of the now defunct *Christian World* once said it was the role of bishops to be concerned 'for little things'. In a letter to the paper, Habgood, then Bishop of Durham, asked: 'If that was the case, whose role is it to be concerned for big things?' He has always been concerned with big issues. And there are plenty of loose screws in the Church needing a theological spanner. Habgood will continue tightening the debate – whether the Church heeds or forbears!

Finally, there is John Habgood the man. This book is emphatically not a biography. Like immortality, the prerequisite for good biography is death! It is not my objective to diminish the irreducible mysteries of the human personality into prosaic order while the subject inhabits the earth! But a mind is not disembodied. It belongs to the man and it had a nursery and a training. So the first two chapters of the book *are* largely biographical, dealing with Habgood's life and development up to the time of his ordination. Thereafter my concern is with themes, issues and subjects.

Nevertheless, the reader is bound to catch at some of the shifting dimensions within which John Habgood lives, thinks, dreams and serves. The perceptive words of Eric Heaton, Dean of Christ Church, Oxford and a former Dean of Durham, help to get the subject of this study in focus. Eric Heaton saw John Habgood in action at Durham, the one as Dean, the other as Bishop.

> He gave me the pleasure of watching a first-class analytical mind at work on a whole range of issues (many of them exceedingly humdrum). I think he has three great strengths: intellectual honesty, skill in analysis, and good judgement of what in particular circumstances is possible. His mental cooling-system is highly efficient; he is not the kind of man who thrashes about in existential *angst*.
>
> Those who expect small-talk from a bishop understandably criticize him for not having any. But they are wrong in suggesting that this proves him to be a cold fish (cool customer, yes: but that's different). When he is intellectually engaged, he is not only animated but accessible (even warm) as a person. He is best, therefore, with those who have questions and problems. I think this detachment is a basic feature of his personality (my guess is that he has never had many intimate friends) and not part of a deliberately imposed discipline, but it does undoubtedly effect an economy of effort and save a lot of nervous energy for other things. One gets the impression that he never hangs about or wastes a moment.
>
> His most secret place, I suspect, is that corner of his life where he enjoys poetry. I often heard him use it devotionally at Auckland Castle, when rural deans or what-have-you were meeting. His own style seems to me clear and civilized but completely lacking in music or imagination. I think probably his sermons are best on tricky *special* occasions, when he is challenged to confront directly the issue raised. On regular church festivals in the Cathedral at Durham, he seemed less at ease. He took the view (about which I got into my only unprofitable argument with him) that ordinary preaching was not for religious instruction but supplementary to the liturgy, to which it should be firmly subordinated. His talks to children are in a class by themselves and seem to reflect a combination of his

appreciation of poetry and fantasy with his love of carpentry, models and toys. I wonder if he finds adults a bit boring.

I always suppose without further inquiry that he shares my theological liberalism, but I don't really *know* where he stands in relation to traditional orthodoxy. The fact that I don't really know illustrates how circumspect he is at revealing what he decides to reveal and *no more*. This is all part of his acute awareness of the context – his practice of *episcope* as the art of the possible.

Living with paradox, struggling with ambiguity are realities, not clichés, for John Habgood. To some extent I am inviting you to share in an adventure of wrestling with words and meanings and symbols. But it is well-earthed, for in the end Christianity is not a heap of phrases but a way of looking at life and living it out.

Habgood once quoted St Hilary, who was writing about early controversies on the creeds: 'We are compelled to attempt what is unattainable, to climb where we cannot reach, to speak what we cannot utter. Instead of the bare adoration of faith we are compelled to entrust the deep things of religion to the perils of human expression.' *This* is an appropriate point of departure, for Habgood is constantly trying to find new ways of conveying the unsayable – hence poetry is very important to him. As he has said: 'Poetry is the enlargement of the imagination and sensibilities – hence part of the groundwork of prayer. (Poetry) puts new life into familiar symbols – unifying experience into a pattern of meaning.' And poetry and symbol alike are just two of the aids for one who has been publicly charged to be or to become 'humble, just and true'.

1

A Letter to God

26 June [1935] Calverton House
Stony Stratford
Bucks.

Dear God,
If you feel lonely up in the sky would you like to come down and stay with us, you could sleep in the spier-room, and you could bathe with us, and I think you would enjoy yourself.
Love from John

The letter, written by eight-year-old John Habgood, was put in an envelope, correctly stamped and posted and addressed to 'Our Father which art in Heaven'. The local postmaster, presumably not the intended recipient, opened it and returned the envelope and contents to John Habgood's father. The envelope was marked 'Return to sender'; thus there were no theological implications as would have arisen had the envelope been marked 'Gone away' or 'Unknown at this address'.

If this suggests a pious and priggish little boy, then such a notion can be dispelled by glancing at his background and early life. Thoughtful and serious – yes! Pious and priggish – no!

John Habgood was fortunate in the circumstances of his background. His father, Arthur Henry Habgood, was born at Eastbourne in 1882. He was educated at Dover College; Jesus College, Cambridge; and the London Hospital from which he qualified in 1908. There was never any doubt that he would be a doctor. His own father, Henry Habgood, had been one of Eastbourne's most prominent general practitioners. The son was gathered up in the First World War as captain in the Special Reserve of the Royal Army Medical Corps and he went to France in mid-August 1914 with the British Expeditionary Force. He was with the Third Division during the retreat from Mons, serving on the Western Front and reaching the rank of Lieutenant-Colonel. He was wounded in 1918, mentioned in dispatches and awarded the DSO the following year.

The basic ingredients in Dr Habgood's character did not alter over the years. He was a steady man with a strong sense of duty. Integrity was recognized in this careful, cautious, bookish doctor. It showed in his actions but was never paraded. It is such men as he – sincere, unaffected, unambitious, unshakably loyal to their principles – who are often the salt of society.

Dr Habgood's first practice was at Coltishall in Norfolk. He had been a house physician of the Victoria Hospital for Children. After the war he went to Rumania where as medical director of the Red Cross child welfare services his work was acclaimed. Indeed, he was responsible for starting infant welfare services in that country and became a friend of Queen Marie.

Back in England in general practice he was well respected, a kind of A. J. Cronin's 'Dr Cameron'. He was more firm than affable, but it was a firmness born of reticence rather than grimness.

In 1922 he left Norfolk for Stony Stratford in Buckinghamshire where he entered a partnership, which, after amalgamation in 1924, became Bull, Habgood and Gooch. That was not all that amalgamated in 1924.

One of Dr Habgood's previous patients was Edgar Hutton, a man with colourful antecedents and a lavish supply of Irish blood in his veins and character. His father had married the daughter of the Earl of Charleville whose family name was Bury. One of the family was Charles Kenneth Howard Bury, who led the Mount Everest Expedition in 1921 before dwelling in the lower reaches of Parliament as Unionist

Member first for the Bilston Division of South Wolverhampton and then for Chelmsford.

Edgar Hutton worked for Mann Egerton for a few years and lived in various country houses in Norfolk. In 1909, in the grotto of Charleville Castle, he proposed marriage to an attractive, lively girl of nineteen. Place and gesture alike were significant of character and manner. The girl was Vera Chetwynd-Stapylton, the youngest daughter of a large family. The Chetwynds and Stapyltons had had separate lineages. They were old families, conscious of their history. Sir Bryan Stapylton was one of the first Knights of the Garter. There was little of particular distinction about recent holders of the titles. At an early age Vera, who was usually known as Poppy, was sent to live with relatives, the Abel-Smiths, in large, rented country houses in Leicestershire and Nottinghamshire. She was brought up, with May Abel-Smith, by governesses.

In 1909 Vera was married to Edgar Hutton. There were two children of the marriage: Dorothy (known as Bunny) born in 1910, and William (Bill) born in 1914. Edgar Hutton lived the life of a country landowner, hunting, shooting and fishing in Norfolk. In January 1924 he was accidentally shot in the foot and died of tetanus. On one of his post-war visits to Norfolk, Dr Habgood remet Hutton's widow and after a short if intermittent courtship they were married in September 1924.

It was a marriage partnership of contrasts. On the one hand was the prudent practitioner who believed that money had to be earned and who held a position in the community which could not be bought; on the other hand was a generous, expansive, exciting, vivacious woman, full of life, who seemed to believe that money came in with the morning milk. It was not that she was a spendthrift. It was simply that her own background had not introduced her to how the other nine-tenths of people lived.

A general practitioner is in a good position to know and to care; and caring usually leads to service. This is one thing they had in common. Dr and Mrs Habgood were people who got things done: the one by stealth, the other by sheer hard work and enthusiasm. They lived at Calverton House in Stony Stratford, Buckinghamshire. Stony Stratford was a town of 4,000 inhabitants and it was here that much of the work was done. Mrs Habgood was a marvellous organizer. 'Good works' is often a term of suspicion, even abuse. But it usually means that someone is deliberately doing good where there is real need. Mrs Habgood ran an Infant Welfare Centre and was at different times President, Hon. Secretary, and Chairman of the local active branch of the British Legion. During the war, with unflagging zeal, she ran the WVS canteen at Stony Stratford. It was an oasis for the convoys of troops moving up and down the A5 who met there for sleep and refreshment. If there was a flag day, Mrs Habgood was usually the one who organized it. John Habgood's earliest memory is of selling flags!

Over the years, from their marriage in 1924 until they left Stony Stratford in 1950, the Habgoods used their gifts, influence and position in the service of the community. Yet they also thoroughly enjoyed themselves. They never emotionally exhausted themselves in the causes they served so that there was nothing left to give to their family.

Mrs Habgood had brought two children to the marriage to which were now added Pamela, born in October 1925, and John Stapylton, the subject of this study, born 23 June 1927. There was rarely any conflict between the children of Mrs Habgood's first marriage and that of her second. They were brothers and sisters together in what was a happy and carefree home. It was a united family. As Pamela has remarked, 'You always knew you were loved'. Although there was help in the house, the children had to work – wash up, clean their rooms, and do other household duties – and these were not regarded as chores. In many ways it was an ideal childhood. There was a streak of strictness and some rigid rules which had to be obeyed, but 'knowing where they were' and where the boundaries were drawn on a few important matters left the children to grow and develop freely to the extent that they were allowed to lead their own lives.

John Habgood was self-contained as a child. He was content with his duties and his pleasures and the latter were simple ones. There was no need for conflict and there was nothing to rebel against. A former companion, Mrs Barbara Weeks, remembers the beautiful house with house and kitchen staff: 'Mrs Habgood always polished the drawing-room before breakfast. There was a large garden with a lot of trees, a tennis court and a river at the bottom of the garden. There was also a rowing-boat in which the children and I spent many hours exploring the reeds, etc. and finding reed warblers' nests with cuckoos in them. More often than not, a dog or even a rabbit would come with us.' It was a mixture of *Swallows and Amazons* and *Children of the New Forest*. Holidays were spent in Norfolk or Swanage, in a caravan or a tent. If there was anything odd about John Habgood's childhood, it was that he eschewed meat and would only eat potatoes and gravy.

Religion in the Habgood household was dutiful, not earnest. The family went to the local church, but it seemed to be more as a natural expression of their position in the place than of active commitment. Parish fêtes and occasions were held in the Habgoods' garden.

As for education, John Habgood went first to a small private school in Stony Stratford run by a Miss E. Y. Stockings. His only report, for the Christmas term 1935, shows him to have been highest in the class at most subjects.

In 1936 he went to boarding school at Hill Brow, Meads, Eastbourne. His sister Pamela went to the Roman Catholic Convent School of Jesus and Mary, Thornton College, Bletchley. Hill Brow was a small school of about forty pupils, with seven full-time and four part-time staff. Habgood worked well, was an evident joy to teach, and his reports were uniformly good. It is clear that at this early age he had a scholastic inclination, but his weakness was English: 'Sound but not inspiring. He must improve both the quality and the quantity of his reading', was the headmaster's comment. Habgood was much more interested in doing things with his hands – for example, making a tuck box – than reading books. Mathematics was his strongest subject. The intention was that he should take a scholarship for Eton. It was almost unknown for a boy who did not show a very considerable proficiency in Greek to win an Eton scholarship: Habgood's translation in Latin, Greek and French left almost everything to be desired, and his English style remained stodgy. The former was due to poor memory, the latter to comparative lack of reading.

In his last year at Hill Brow, Habgood was Head Boy. He was not a success. The headmaster, F. J. H. Matthews, wrote to his father (1 August 1939): 'It has seemed to me that some of the older, though junior, boys have not taken too kindly to his being over them and at the same time he has not received as much support as he should from the others at the top of the School . . . I think, too, the exercise of a little more tact on his part will make his path smoother.'

The picture that emerges is no longer one of the carefree, contented child but of a studious, struggling, serious boy, not making friends easily or being much bothered about making them at all. His school reports may carry criticism but he was nonetheless always top of his class and he was a year younger than the average boys in his class.

Habgood was evacuated from Hill Brow in 1939, at the age of twelve, for The Knoll, Woburn Sands. In a class of four the sole purpose was to prepare him for the Common Entrance Examination to Eton. Here the surprisingly large gaps in his Latin and Greek were plugged. In literature he was propelled in a critical direction, beginning to see the difference between the good and the second-rate. Above all, in the two years he was at The Knoll his character developed in ways that have not significantly changed. In retrospect some comments of headmasters appear banal or shortsighted when they are not plainly irrelevant. In this case those of headmaster I. A. Zair are perceptive and stand the microscopic test of time. At various stages he wrote of Habgood: 'General attitude – combines modesty and seriousness of purpose with a keen sense of humour'. 'An observant boy possessing initiative, quiet confidence and plenty of common sense.' 'His artistic and mathematical leaning give him a good mental balance.' 'His keen observation and sense of humour enable him to preserve discipline in quite the right spirit and with a minimum of effort.'

Habgood was successful in the examination, went to Eton in 1941 and was placed in Remove, which was the highest form possible for him at that stage. However, as we shall see, Habgood was not *naturaliter Etonica*! Eton is a major planet, not a minor star, and is not easily comprehended by those outside its galaxy. It is one of the most misunderstood institutions in the land, for it is as much an institution as a school. It has ever generated confidence and ambition in its inmates: generally the sons of the privileged, pleasured and financially possessed. It is not a repository for the sons of gentlefolk but more of a junior club for the influential-elect. The educational atmosphere has always inculcated a sense of camaraderie enjoyed by its scholars and feared by its adversaries. It is all in 'The Eton Boating Song', both the tune and the words:

> Rugby may be more clever,
> Harrow may make more row,
> But we'll swing together,
> Steady from stroke to bow.
> And nothing on earth can sever
> The chain that is round us now.

Eton encouraged a sane and orderly mind running on practical rather than speculative or abstract lines. It was much, perhaps more, the atmospheric embrace of Eton than the quality of education which manufactured leaders. Some men possess an inbred superiority which gives them a dominating influence over their contemporaries and marks them out unmistakably for leadership. As Aristotle said: 'Those who think themselves worthy of great things, they *are* worthy.' On this basis Habgood was anything but a natural fit for the Eton mould.

In considering Habgood's time at Eton from 1941 to 1945, it is important to remember that it was during the war. One of Habgood's contemporaries at Eton, Lord Wrenbury, recaptures the feeling of entering Eton in 1941:

> It was a pretty frightening experience for a boy, even if he had been to a boarding school previously. Long leaves had been done away with on the outbreak of war, and there were no facilities for telephoning parents, which meant that for most new boys the only way of keeping in touch was through long anguished letters and the comforting bulky envelopes from our mothers in reply. Petrol of course was in short supply, the weekly ration being equivalent to about

> thirty miles, so for most of us the only hope of a parental visit during term-time depended upon the practicality or otherwise of transport by bus or train. There was no question of a boy being allowed away for the night, and the number of parents able to get to Eton and back for the pleasure of one afternoon's reunion must have been quite small.

Getting accustomed to the Etonian environment is not easy. For someone like Habgood who had not the advantage of arriving at Eton from a school which specialized in sending boys to Eton, such as Summerfields or the Dragon School, the initial reception and personal encounters were stony, sharp and bleak. Lord Wrenbury thinks one of the strengths of the Eton system 'is that one very soon finds one's place in society'.

> Though the school as a whole amounted to about 1,100 boys, each boys' house contained only about forty and within that small community there was a well-defined hierarchy. At the top were the boys in the Library – an elective body usually comprising the seven or eight boys in their last year. They alone were entitled to be served by fags. Below them was a body called Debate, a peculiar institution apparently without privileges because debates were seldom if ever held. Below them again was a class known as Upper Boys whose great claim to fame was that they had outgrown the fagging system, and below them were the Lower Boys who were still subject to it.

The house system worked well if you happened to be in a good house. Almost everything depended on the housemaster, whose personal influence was paramount. People destined for leadership, though not necessarily greatness (which is a very different matter), were marked from birth. Boys were entered for a particular house at birth when the dominant factor would have been the housemaster's relationship with the parents. Lord Wrenbury continues:

> Each house was distinguished by a particular ethos. In John's time two were particularly noted for their snobbish side in the sense that most of the boys with titles gravitated

to one or other of them; three or four were particularly outstanding for their games-playing ability. Some houses were definitely regarded as 'tough' and others as civilized. One had a reputation for vulgarity while another had a reputation for being well-fed (all food was provided at the housemaster's personal expense and in this particular case the housemaster was a wealthy bachelor).

John's house was by common consent regarded as a dim house, in the sense that very few of the boys there ever made much of an impression on the rest of the school and few of them were elected to POP, that exclusive society membership of which demonstrated unusual popularity or athletic distinction and the privileges of which included the right to wear braided tails, a winged collar, fancy waistcoat, and pepper-and-salt trousers. The house itself was situated away from the centre of things not far from the school boundary. It had a dank and depressing appearance as though there were a shortage of daylight inside. The boys for the most part were correspondingly scruffy. As one of them, a major-general, said afterwards, 'We never had a very good reputation; if a boy was caught smoking or cheating in trials it was most likely to be one of Mr Mayes's boys.' But for all that, the boys seem to have become fond of their housemaster once they got to know him.

The housemaster of the domain of the dims was Charles Mayes. His was a house where scientists dwelled, and science was the Cinderella of the Eton curriculum. Those who did science tended not to do Greek, and Greek appeared to provide the watershed between those who were considered bright and those who were not. The reason Habgood was placed in this house, and probably the reason he was at Eton at all, was due to the fact that the Dame of the house was a relative of Mrs Habgood! Although Habgood did not get a scholarship, Charles Mayes took Habgood into his house at a greatly reduced cost. He had read the reports on Habgood, thought they were good and hoped he might raise the academic temperature of the house.

Before we consider Habgood's record and achievements, we shall ask how a contemporary saw him.

> He was not remarkable in any way except perhaps for the fact that, notwithstanding the general mediocrity and forgettability of most others in his house, we all knew and liked him. He was thin and tall but not excessively so, and his expression was pleasant and friendly. He seemed to be a fish that had somehow swum into the wrong pool. The word that springs most readily to mind is 'gangling'; his tailcoat hung upon his slightly drooping shoulders as upon a loosely limbed scarecrow, but for all that he was always neat and tidy. He was gentle and not forceful and one who seemed destined to pass through his school career in decent obscurity. There were some we were sure who were destined for great things but our boyish prescience was singularly lacking in John's case though we might possibly have been able to see him in the role of an absent-minded professor.
>
> Had he been in another house, things might have been different. Had he gone into College it would probably have been the best thing of all. He cannot have found many kindred spirits at Mr Mayes's and however formidable his own mental equipment no one can afford to miss out on the stimulus of friendship and intellectual activity which Eton is pre-eminently capable of providing under the right conditions.

These latter sentiments betray a misunderstanding of Habgood. Some of the stimulus of Eton hinged on such words as action, movement, battles, manoeuvres, noise, conflict, heartiness, games. Many of Habgood's contemporaries were articulate and effervescent. Their talk was worldly, political and intelligent but with a good deal of froth on the surface and not always with much down the deep well on which to draw. Habgood was not like that. He continued to be self-contained and appeared to be self-sufficient. He was a little buttoned-up, though neither intense nor repressed.

Basically Habgood was very serious-minded and through steady and determined industry he worked his way to the top in many subjects. Charles Mayes would see him 'working and reading in his room at night'. This was not because he needed to work extra hard to 'keep up', but rather because he found the studious life conducive. Thirty years later, whenever he was picked up by his chauffeur for evening meetings in Durham, the light would go on in the back of the car and he (then Bishop of Durham) would be immersed in a book or the latest issue of a scientific periodical before he had left the courtyard of Auckland Castle. He remains a natural student.

At Eton Habgood was quiet, so oral contributions to any subject were slight. But his reports and the testimony of others show a significant development of sharpness of observation and critical ability in interpretation. It is a character trait. He tells so little of his private thoughts that few realize that his eyes see a very great deal. And what he sees with his eyes and absorbs through his antennae is stored at the bottom of the well for future use.

Habgood's written work was clearly expressed and consistently to the point, but it still lacked imagination. Occasionally a master would hope for a sparkling essay but had to be content with a thoroughly competent and intelligent piece of work. Habgood's powers of perception and mental alacrity were praised. For one who was cautious, probably too cautious, and given to understatement, it is amusing to find a comment in a history report alleging 'several bad exaggerations' in 'a recent answer on allied mistakes in the last war'. It was not a charge that could easily be pressed against him in the future. An interesting comment comes from L. Gordon Whitby (now Professor of Clinical Chemistry in the University of Edinburgh): 'At Eton we were undoubtedly rivals in that we both had our sights on the Moseley Prize for Physics. John is a year younger than I am, but I think he had a better understanding of Physics and I remember being rather in awe of his grasp of the principles of the subject. Also I retain clear impressions of his industry and quiet determination. I would go so far as to say that I was, perhaps, a little afraid of John.'

If study absorbed most of Habgood's time, it did not account for all of it. There was time for some outdoor activities. As Senior Wet Bob he took a great deal of trouble on the river. He was a keen member (eventually Senior Member for his house) in the Junior Training Corps and in 1945 took his house into the final of the Section Cup to finish second by one mark. Charles Mayes wrote to Habgood's father (August 1945): 'To win the willing co-operation of every member of the section and command them as he did showed a capacity for leadership of a very high order.' Accordingly Habgood was responsible for raising the standards of his house in this and academic ways so that it was no longer regarded as a place where dim boys resided!

However, Eton did not give Habgood an ardent enthusiasm for a cause or a discriminating sympathy for individuals. His social sympathies were not strong and his political interests were not keen.

One final aspect of Eton life has to be mentioned. The religion of the College chapel was uninspired and uninspiring. Occasionally a visiting preacher would sparkle the senses or enrich the mind. More often, the opposite was what Habgood found on offer. As a matter of routine he was confirmed as a member of the Church of England. It was not a turning-point, not even a milestone. What did it all mean? He had absorbed the undemanding religion of his home without effort and without challenge or serious thought. Such religion is easily shed. Before he left Eton, Habgood had not only shed his religious remnant but thrown it away. In its place was not apathy but atheism. Perhaps there was more veneer than substance in his professed atheism. Nevertheless, he had abandoned his belief and practice of the Christian religion.

In 1945 he left Eton for King's College, Cambridge. He went to do physics but the Director of Studies at King's wanted to broaden the base of those undergraduates whose chosen subjects were mathematics, physics or chemistry and he persuaded Habgood to do physiology. Habgood had taken a scholarship and failed, but instead won a State Bursary. In the July examination he was awarded an Oppidan Prize and the Moseley Physics and Chemistry prizes.

2

Divine Nudge

The King's College, Cambridge of 1945 was bleak. Some of the academic glories had or were about to depart by death or promotion. Keynes and Clapham died in 1946 and Milner-White had already gone to be Dean of York. Life in the College was rigorous and was to become more so when, for example, bread was rationed in July 1946 for the first time. It had been exempted during the hostilities as a safety valve against possible panic about starvation as a result of enemy action.

In *A Century of Kings 1873–1972* Patrick Wilkinson captures the 1945 intake:

> The veterans who began to come up or return in 1945 were not, as had been feared, a shell-shocked generation. They were mostly men matured by experience whose chief aim seemed to be to get a 'war degree' in the abbreviated time permitted and then get on with the business of life. Not that they were bookworms: far from it. . . Among those returning were men who had come up for short courses as wartime cadets. These were of two kinds: men who had been accepted in the normal way and been deferred, mostly winners of Scholarships and Exhibitions, and men selected by the Forces. The College gave all of them a chance to return, and the latter class at least did something to broaden its catchment area.

Habgood belonged to another category of newcomers, namely those straight from public or grammar school. Normally, young men were doing their National Service, but the government was encouraging those who were studying physics, chemistry and mathematics to undertake the university courses instead. In this way the government hoped to be the beneficiary by recruiting graduate scientists for research and development in such subjects as radar.

Science required a greater commitment of time than other subjects. There were lectures all morning and practicals all afternoon. Undergraduates worked alone for long hours. Habgood had little money to spend on entertainment and was never an *habitué* of the pub, standing at bars talking and drinking endlessly and aimlessly. He much preferred to go to Marshall's aircraft dump and buy bits of surplus electrical and other equipment.

There were gruelling moments! Habgood was almost unnerved when by private arrangement he did a term's dissection in the Anatomy School. He had to dissect premature babies which were stored in a great tank, like an aquarium. There they were, dead babies floating in green liquid in the tank.

Habgood gained first-class honours in parts i and ii of the Natural Science Tripos in 1947 and 1948 respectively. His performance in the finals won him a grant to do research in neurophysiology on nerve tissues, under the general direction of Bryan Matthews, whose research was instrumental in making possible high-altitude flight and who made major advances in the sphere of electrophysiology. In 1952 Matthews was appointed Professor of Physiology at Cambridge, a post he held until 1973. He was knighted in 1952 and died on 22 July 1986. It was clear to Matthews that the good student would be a good teacher. It was teaching by learning, for Habgood started teaching as soon as he graduated, beginning with students from Downing College and Girton College. Moreover, Habgood thoroughly enjoyed teaching. Matthews was anxious to get Habgood's teaching abilities retained for medical students but there was no vacancy on the staff of King's to which he could be appointed. However, through the auspices of the Professor of Pharmacology, C. Verney, a new post was created whereby Habgood spent mornings teaching students in pharmacology and continued his physiological research in the afternoon.

Habgood's research was very promising, though of a basic nature far from early application to practical medicine. It was research into pain, investigating the effect of electrical impulses on certain nerves affecting the tenderness of the skin. The physiologist is concerned, among other things, with the physical basis of sensation; it is his job to tell us how information about the outside world is gathered by our sense-organs, our eyes, ears, skin, etc. and then conveyed to and used by the brain. The area in which Habgood researched concerned the heightened sensitivity to pain caused by injury, the technical term for which is hyperalgesia. His experiments, mostly on frogs and rats, entailed applying shocks to one nerve and observing the appearance of the impulse in another nerve. He carried out a number of experiments on his own arm, with mingled results. Sometimes he obtained hyperalgesia but more often he did not, as witness a not untypical diary entry: '(1 July 1950). Did expts on my arm – not very successful attempt to anaesthetize nerve. Found no change of threshold, but could not get good hyperalgesia – too painful.' His thesis, for which he was awarded a doctorate in philosophy in 1952, was 'Hyperalgesia – An Electrophysiological Approach'.

Habgood's work was a small brick in a structure he and others were building towards an understanding of the physical nature of pain. Professor Matthews recalls that Habgood's 'interest in neurophysiology was clear in many discussions we had on research on the nervous system and brain'. He adds:

> I may have communicated my own scepticism that intellectual processes could reach a full understanding of reality. I see no paradox between science and religion. In the brain we have a computing system, abstracting rules under which the physical world operates, and this enables man (and, in varying degrees, animals too) to predict the probable course of events and so take action to forestall them, thus giving a brain power to shape its future environment. It is no longer a plaything of inevitable physical forces.

Richard Adrian (now Lord Adrian, Master of Pembroke College, Cambridge) did Part ii of the Natural Sciences Tripos in Physiology with Habgood in 1947–8. They worked closely together and Lord Adrian remembers that year as being 'intellectually enormously stimulating and exciting and that much of the excitement came from being one of a small group of congenial and dedicated colleagues and in a laboratory which was just beginning to see that scientific problems abandoned at the beginning of the war could be taken up again. Many new lines were starting in the late forties and early fifties and it was hard to see which of them would lead on to major advances. In the event it was intercellular recording with glass capillary microelectrodes which dominated investigations of the central nervous mechanisms for the quarter century following the end of the Second World War'. With this hindsight Lord Adrian thinks Habgood's papers had an almost pre-war flavour and seemed to address with established methods unresolved questions of the inter-war years. However, he thinks that 'had Habgood continued in physiology he would have contributed a great deal to work on the cellular mechanisms of transmission of the spinal cord'. Two of Habgood's papers were published in the *Journal of Physiology:* 'Sensitization of sensory receptors in the frog's skin' (1950) and 'Antidromic impulses in the dorsal roots' (1953).

Any young scientist tends to be mesmerized by science. His work is not cold, abstract, impersonal, mechanical. It is often intensely exciting: he may be passionately concerned in it; it may inspire in him the highest kinds of devotion and self-sacrifice; and it may be emotionally satisfying. The world of the arts is wrongly contrasted with that of science as if one were versatile and exhilarating and the other mechanical and dull. Perhaps the inner glow in the scientist does not always radiate a bright countenance. He can appear cold and intense. Appearances are notoriously misleading, yet there is a measure of accuracy in the conveyed impression. Habgood was an example of this.

The view of science based on Habgood's practice of it is that actual advance is slow, factual and anti-speculative. Theory should be only half a step ahead of fact. When the gap between theory and fact widens, the results can be devastating as, for example, in uncontrolled and seemingly uncontrollable experiments. In later chapters we will consider and analyse Habgood's scientific approach to specific scientific and medical issues of our time.

One who knew him better than most at Cambridge was Dr R. E. D. Clark, who had taken his Ph.D in organic chemistry in 1932 and had stayed up at Cambridge teaching and researching. Dr Clark started a Science and Religion Society with E. J. Ambrose (now a professor) and edited a periodical, *Science and Religion*, which had a small, lively and esoteric readership. Habgood lived with Dr and Mrs Clark for two and a half years. They called him 'Happy', because of his observable contentment rather than his inner tranquillity, for he was neither easygoing nor relaxed. 'John was always extremely Etonian in his manners – ultra polite. At meals, if you asked if he would like some more of a dish, he would always refuse. Ask again and he would always refuse again. But ask a third time and he would always (or nearly always) say, "Well, perhaps I will after all!" '

Dr Clark recalls Habgood's poetic mind and sense of fun: for example, describing mathematical formulae in scientific papers as if they had come to life and were on a solemn march. 'But I did not think he was at all like the usual run of scientists. He seemed to fight shy of anything controversial. Once I bought some dimethylthanolamine from the chemist, turned it into the tartrate then started eating it as a possible brain stimulant. Thought it might interest Happy as an extra methyl group lands you with an important nerve chemical, coline. But Happy was horrified. I think that perhaps he was a bit bored with science: he never talked about the work he was doing or showed the slightest interest in the scientific papers I had published.'

Dr Clark is only half wrong. There is not one single view of science. Clark's adventurousness was not Habgood's, yet his approach was no less compelling. Writing some years later on 'The attractiveness of science' (*Theology*, 1958), Habgood wrote forcefully:

> The most important truth for the non-scientist to realize about science is that the scientist sees himself as committed, not so much to a particular body of theory, as to a particular method. Theory will change and can change because the scientific method is self-correcting. Philosophical questions can be left to sort themselves out and do not greatly disturb the average scientist. The method is

the central characteristic of science, and theology stands condemned because it does not seem to employ it.

Contrary to popular assumption the scientiest is simple-minded. He chooses the simplest explanation to explain a phenomenon. He likes order. This can lead to the creation of a kingdom of the mind in which order is law. Everything – perhaps everyone – in the kingdom can be conveniently labelled. The observable result is sometimes the superiority, even the arrogance, of the scientific approach. It helps to know that everything can be accounted for and that everyone is in a recognizable slot. Such may be the view from outside but inside the kingdom one observer is as good as another. 'The scientist's authority is no greater than the repeatableness of his results.'

One of Habgood's earliest published articles was 'Physiology for the medical student' which appeared in the *Cambridge University Medical Society Magazine* (27 (3) Easter Term, 1950). He made the point that physiology was an independent science, no longer a branch of medicine. Perhaps he first learnt the message, though not yet the richness, of compromise, through physiology:

> The method of science is to isolate systems as much as possible, for the more completely the conditions of an experiment can be specified, the more reliable are the conclusions drawn from it. On the other hand, the more we isolate a physiological system, the less likely is it to function physiologically. In practice physiologists have to compromise, but are not always careful to point out just how much their experiment may have upset the normal functioning of the system they are studying.

In that article there were shades of the future too. An 'attitude of constant appeal to verifiable facts, and the elimination of as many assumptions as possible, should act as a valuable antidote to the unavoidable empiricism of practical medicine'. And, more important still, 'As we begin to develop the scientific method of thought, and as we learn to assess the relevance and trustworthiness of facts, so will we teach ourselves the art of judgement. As we recognize the limitations and insignificance of our knowledge, so should we recapture something of an attitude of wonder. And as we learn to criticize, so should we learn humility.'

Habgood seemed destined for a life of research and teaching at Cambridge. Any thoughts he may have once had for following the tradition of his family by becoming a general practitioner had long since vanished.

Turning from science to religion, we recall that Habgood left Eton for Cambridge an atheist. In the autumn of 1946 there was an Evangelical Mission in Cambridge led by Dr Donald Barnhouse. He was a Presbyterian minister from Philadelphia who had a considerable reputation as a missioner. His preaching was as challenging as his appeal was direct. But, like all such well-organized missions the meetings and services were somewhat contrived and controlled as bait to hook fish. Revivalist hymns, the encouragement of emotions, professional testimonies, an emphasis on sin and the need to be saved were the staple fare on the menu. All manner of means were adopted to entice people to services and informal gatherings.

After the Mission, Habgood noted: 'To an outsider the Mission promised to be great fun. There were unlimited opportunities for having free teas, and to one like myself, who had no fear of being converted, there was the pleasant feeling of being able to adopt a condescending attitude towards those whom one inwardly despises. For hadn't science disproved the existence of God? Wasn't Christianity outmoded and impracticable? At any rate it didn't work – that was obvious even within my own experience.'

A meeting was arranged for all old Etonians at Cambridge. It did not matter whether the old Etonians were agnostic, atheist, lukewarm or boiling-hot Christians: they were all invited, and Habgood was one of that number. He had no overwhelming desire to go, but the meeting happened to fall on one of his bridge evenings. Although he enjoyed bridge, his regular partner, Peter Swinnerton-Dyer (now Chairman of the University Grants Commission), was becoming increasingly tiresome as he thought each game should be followed by a post-mortem. The interminable post-mortems appeared to have become the reason for the game and Habgood decided to escape by attending the meeting.

Among the people he met was Major W. F. Batt, one of the organizers of the Mission. Major Batt was a country landowner in Norfolk, a former Guards Officer and member of the Church Assembly of the Church of England. He was a 'straight up-and-down Christian' for whom God was his Commanding Officer. There was much Bible talk that left Habgood unimpressed. He could not understand how seemingly good minds could be so uncritically shallow and closed when swallowing the Bible, whole. However, he was persuaded to attend one of the main Mission meetings. What had he to lose? Or rather, as he put it: 'From want of something better to do, along I went to Great St Mary's.' While recognizing Dr Barnhouse's forceful personality in the pulpit, Habgood was amused rather than convinced. It was entertainment. For a joke he filled in a little form after the service was over to arrange an interview with Dr Barnhouse for the following day. 'Wild thoughts of converting him floated through my mind, and I spent a happy evening drawing up a list of unanswerable questions.

> It was with considerable self-confidence that I presented myself at the vestry of Great St Mary's the next day, and Dr Barnhouse's first remarks did nothing to encourage me. He leant very close and with his face almost touching mine said, 'Are you saved?' Phew! How could we talk about the evolution of dinosaurs after an opening gambit like that? And so for the next hour and a half it was he who chose the topics for discussion. Though very little of what he said convinced me, I remember being impressed by one fact, his obvious sincerity, and realized that however absurd his belief might be it was intensely real to him.

Two days before the end of the Mission Habgood received a note asking him if he would like to meet Dr Barnhouse again. Habgood's inclination was to say 'no' as he was rather tired of the Mission, its free teas and fringe activities. However, he somehow found himself going to see Dr Barnhouse in his room.

There was Dr Barnhouse and off we plunged into the same old arguments that I had indulged in for years. I was sick and tired of it all, but somehow desperately I had to salvage my pride and self-assurance. And so on for an hour, of attack and counter-attack, argument and counter-argument, until Barnhouse suddenly changed his tactics. Instead of arguing he told me a few simple stories of how God had worked in his own life – and then, wisely, he sent me away. My thoughts as I went out were chaotic: he believed it . . . it worked for him . . . he was sincere, desperately sincere . . . but was it true? Oh God, was it true?'

I suppose I was converted even before I reached the bottom of the staircase, but it was in Great St Mary's that evening before the service began that I really gave myself to God.

The date was 28 November 1946.

The following evening Habgood was with Major Batt, drinking tea in the lounge of the Blue Boar Hotel. Some undergraduates nearby were arguing in a similar way to his the evening before. How silly it all seemed now. 'Why don't you tell them so?' said Major Batt. Habgood remembers how, with his 'stomach resting rather uneasily somewhere down in the coal cellar below, I got up and started to make a speech and eventually I stopped too. I have never felt such a fool, but it did me good. I had burnt my boats.'

From that moment he was gathered up in a relentless, bustling round of Bible-study groups and prayer meetings. He studied and learned the Bible and very soon had a text for most occasions, answers for the doubters and warnings for the waverers. The Cambridge Inter-Collegiate Christian Union, known as CICCU, was very strong and its members included those who were later to attain high office in the Churches as well as in other areas of national life. For a few years Habgood's life was lived between the laboratory and the Bible, dissecting rats by day and digesting the Bible at night. Although he did not see it that way, his days were spent peering through a microscope examining objects and studying them with critical faculties alert, but during the evenings his objective approach was put aside in an intellectually superficial study of the Bible. On the one hand there was meticulous research where questions were more important than answers; on the other hand, a book full of answers to most of the tantalizing questions of the day, a position he was to reverse within five years.

The next turning-point came towards the end of 1949. It was not dramatic as his conversion had been. Moreover, it placed the preceding years in a different perspective. Although Habgood's converted heart and physical presence were with his new-found Christ, was his intellect totally committed? He may have written to Major Batt a year after his conversion: 'I have made a point of straightening out all those old scientific and philosophical difficulties which I was so keen on arguing about. How silly they all seem now.' But did they? Was his mind as committed as his heart? Did he surrender his intellect or did he keep something in reserve?

There is paradox here. Habgood's conversion had been liberating for him in all kinds of ways. He could write: 'Life seems to be made up of three overlapping spheres – the intellectual, the aesthetic and the social. Over and above these, exerting a unifying and cohesive action, giving purpose and meaning, lies religion.' There is no doubt that growth in religion led to growth in aesthetic appreciation and social purpose. He began to appreciate art. Shakespeare was rediscovered and poetry and good literature were new companions. His theological reading started with a limited range of Inter-Varsity Fellowship publications and commentaries all carrying the IVF imprimatur: *nihil obstat.* That did not satisfy Habgood for long. Looking at the kind of books he was reading in 1950 we find among them William Temple's *Mens Creatrix*, *Christus Veritas* and *Nature, Man and God* in rapid succession; the *Collected Poems of T. S. Eliot;* and some of the provocatively stimulating works of Dorothy L. Sayers. All these authors have had a permanent influence on him.

As Habgood opened his mind, widened his horizons, broadened his interests and ideas and began to explore, he had to face some inner conflict. It was not the return of atheism; simply, honest doubt. He admitted:

On the one hand I could no longer feel secure or cocksure

> in my beliefs; I was walking on a razor's edge with disaster on either side; it would be so easy to crash over into heresy or worldliness, and many times I was brought back by prayer and wise Christian friends. But on the other hand whole new realms of experience seemed to be flooded with light; I could really begin to feel my way into the minds of others – to grow in sympathy and understanding. I remember a bishop asking, 'Do you love people because you want to convert them, or do you want to convert them because you love them?' I dare not say that I began to love, but at least I began to see how it might be done.

I have said that with his conversion Habgood's life had been changed but not transformed. Now the transformation was beginning to take place. He was taking theology seriously and this led his faith away from the neatly wrapped answer. Theology was a deliverance from that kind of dogmatism, as it constantly opened up the ultimate questions. The overwhelming self-assurance of CICCU adherents was beginning to look like smug superiority and bigotry. It is said that people who are capable of setting people free are also good at enslaving them. Is this what was in danger of happening? Had Christ set Habgood free or enslaved him? The 'simple gospel' began to look like a fiction. Problems could not be prayed away in a CICCU prayer meeting.

What actually levered him away from the evangelicalism he had been professing was a Saturday-night Bible reading where the speaker, a country parson, was talking on 'God the Creator'. Habgood remembers that meeting vividly, and he recorded some notes soon after the meeting:

> He was obviously out of his depth as most of us would be on such a topic; but the disturbing thing was that he showed no signs of realizing it. On the contrary he began discussing contemporary scientific thought in a most arrogant fashion, and finally dismissed the theory of evolution with a joke about Darwin's personal appearance – 'And the man even looked like a monkey.' And the really shattering thing was that the audience laughed – not at him, but with him. This was Cambridge, a centre of the intellectual life; this was a group of young men, the intellectual élite

> of Evangelicalism, who were prepared to dismiss staggering problems with a laugh, a pious phrase or a scripture text. It was a revelation to me. I began to see for the first time the closed mind in operation. It was as though there was a citadel of belief beyond the range of ordinary criticism.

It was too much for Habgood. From that moment he severed his links with the diehards, or lightheads, of the Movement. He could never take them seriously again. Nevertheless, his own experience has always made him sensitive to the claims of Evangelicals, even when he thinks some of their assertive positions are untenable. He also thinks that the Evangelicals of his years – Maurice Wood, Norman Anderson, David Sheppard, John Stott – were not as 'hard' as some of the Conservative Evangelicals of today whose consciences reign on many issues but do not rule.

Moreover, for Habgood, who had something of an air of easy superiority about him, this claustrophobic world of testifying, Bible study and mutual preening was not good. Spiritual vanity was fostered by the self-imposed isolation of Evangelicals from the general life of the colleges. The trouble was, they lived too much in one another's society, and thus lost touch with the larger world and wider Church. Hence their lamentable lack of interest in everything save that which they could bring within the orbit of their distinctive and fundamentalist interpretation of Christianity. In an atmosphere so limited and prejudiced, it was but too easy to develop a conceited and censorious spirit. Fortunately the nature of Habgood's own personality saved him from the megalomania of zeal and his gifts in the scientific sphere prevented spiritual egotism.

Unfortunately, some CICCUites appeared to have a thoroughgoing contempt for the individual conscience. Like any proselytizers they sought but one end, the conquest of men and women for Christ, but were in danger of pursuing it with relentless indifference to the moral injury they might incidentally inflict on their converts. CICCU adherents concentrated too much on power and not enough on wisdom. Their meetings were designed to make members better evangelists; to increase their effectiveness in the use of the Bible and to rouse their enthuiasm for greater sacrifice to God; to make them more powerful Christians but not necessarily wiser or more sensitive ones.

Habgood contributed a number of articles to *The Pilgrim Newsletter* (published by the Scripture Union) in 1950 and 1951, on such subjects as 'The scientific attitude', 'Brains', 'On the virtuous life', 'Personality', 'Static or dynamic'. They were free from the worst excesses of Bible-bleating shibboleths, but were lightweight and uncritical. A more interesting article appeared in *Inter-Varsity* (Autumn Term, 1952) on 'Rewards'. By now we see a change of emphasis and some new sources: no longer the reliable evangelical hacks, but St Augustine, C. S. Lewis and Dorothy L. Sayers, are quoted. Some of his evangelical friends criticized him for moving away from the rewards that are mentioned in the New Testament – inheriting the earth, having authority over cities, receiving crowns, sitting on thrones, partaking of the marriage supper of the Lamb, receiving the prize of God's high calling. Habgood contended that individual Christians should be like Christ, finding joy in doing God's will rather than suffering and obeying to obtain some concrete reward. There was a correspondence with Dr R. E. D. Clark in later issues of *Inter-Varsity*, but Habgood was worried about the legal-sounding nature of his opponent's case rather than placing any emphasis on love. He retorted: 'The promise of concrete rewards, which has led us up to the summit of loving union with God, is from there seen as the opportunity for that love to find objective expression. Service, responsibility, honour and power are no longer the precursors of love, but the fruits of it. Even the level of self-indulgence looks different. "Love God," said St Augustine, "and do what you like." '

Habgood had a profitable time as a member of the Research Scientists' Christian Fellowship (associated with IVF). Members at the time included a number who distinguished themselves in their particular discipline: Frank H. T. Rhodes (later Professor of Geology, University College of Swansea), Donald M. MacKay (later Professor of Communication, University of Keele), David E. J. Ingram (later Professor of Physics, University of Keele), Robert L. F. Boyd (later Professor of Physics, University College, London), John C.

Polkinghorne (later Professor of Mathematical Physics, University of Cambridge). A small group was invited by IVF to write a book on science and faith. Habgood wrote the preface and two substantial chapters. The project came to nothing, partly because of the divergences of opinion that were involved but chiefly resulting from Habgood's own outlook which changed during the course of the discussions to a point where he clearly was not in agreement with the other members of the group. Again the stumbling-block was the uncritical biblical orientation of the group. Douglas C. Spanner (later Professor) was a member. Nowhere is the point better illustrated than in Professor Spanner's review of Habgood's *A Working Faith* in *The Churchman* (1980) when he wrote: 'I think my main disappointment with this book arises from its lack of biblical reference, for Dr Habgood speaks in terms of "Christian insights" rather than biblical revelation. To a certain extent he answers this criticism in his Personal Postscript at the end, but the latter left me unconvinced. If "religion is about the unsayable" then what is the New Testament for?'

When Habgood himself held a narrow evangelical, almost fundamentalist, view he was shunned by some fellow scientists who otherwise would have been his friends. Dr Hal Dixon of Cambridge discovered the pitfalls of CICCU earlier than Habgood and recalls: 'I was probably not ready to make friends with anyone who belonged to CICCU, as I had found it a distressing experience to join CICCU on coming up to Cambridge in 1946, and then be faced with demands for loyalty to an organization whose outlook I did not share, as it seemed to me exclusive (I became active in the Student Christian Movement). Towards the end of our time as research students I greatly warmed to John. I remember his telling me not to attribute to him all the views he may have expressed a few years earlier (we were both growing up).'

There was another consequence of Habgood's position during the time of his disengagement from the CICCU embrace. The dons of King's College were not conspicuously Christian and many were avowed atheists, even if they did take part in the annual celebration of the Word made Flesh in as many carols as lessons at Christmastide. Habgood was academically sound and establishing himself as a very promising researcher and a first-rate teacher, yet when his name first went forward for a Fellowship he was rejected on the specific grounds that as an Evangelical he could not be 'intellectually up to it'. He was elected a Fellow in Natural Sciences in 1952. (His former rival, L. G. Whitby, was elected a Fellow in Natural Sciences in 1951.) At King's the annual elections of Fellows from among promising young graduates were *prize* Fellowships, not staff appointments. Habgood had already been appointed Demonstrator in Pharmacology in 1950.

One very good outcome of Habgood's conversion and evangelical contacts was that the news spread. To his surprise students started coming to him with their problems because they thought he would have a sympathetic ear. His reputation as a scientist was already secure. His personality was trusted yet unknown. Now for the first time in his life he was 'discovering people'. He enjoyed teaching and knew his students' academic travails because he had wrestled with most of them himself. Yet up until this time there had been something a little impersonal in his approach, a mite distant in his manner, so that at the point where there was a chance of real personal encounter he remained aloof. But gradually the defences were lowering as he discovered that all these other people were only a 'little lower than the angels' too.

Habgood saw ever more clearly that entering into other people's problems, helping them to find their own directions, required a sensitivity that was both great and selective. In some published broadcast talks entitled 'A Biologist Looks at Life' and given during his Jedburgh ministry, he said:

> Jesus was sensitive. Nobody could care more for people than he. Nobody saw more deeply into the complexities of the human heart; nobody took more seriously the world which God had made. Yet the life of Jesus is remarkable for the number of things he did not do; the questions he left unanswered; the people with whom he had only the most fleeting contact; the needs he had to leave unmet. Sensitive, yet selective. He could bear to leave things, because he trusted God. He attended undistractedly to those who needed him, because he saw their coming as

> part of the will of God. He let the world with all its conflicts and complexities beat upon him without overwhelming him, because louder than any other sound he heard the voice of God.

This will be a recurrent theme for Habgood in the years to come. Becoming 'sensitive, yet selective' was a strong ingredient in his transformation.

There was much debate between Habgood and his colleagues in the Physiology Department as to the purpose of research. Then, in 1950, came the Korean War. The war did not in fact extend beyond Korea; but the first half of the twentieth century ended with both East and West employing the triumphs of modern technology to lay waste an already poor country whose inhabitants were butchered by ideologues on either side among their fellow-countrymen. There was always the possibility of that war leading to nuclear war. With clarity and severity Habgood asked himself: 'If there was a nuclear war and I survived it, what use would I be if all I can do is cut up frogs and rats?' Asking himself that question was the beginning of the journey that was to lead him from Cambridge to York.

During these Cambridge years his diaries are full of references to long conversations, arguments and discussions on most subjects except politics and economics. It was an exceedingly full life. There was a good deal of public speaking, letters to newspapers (published and unpublished), attending conferences, and leading groups at boys' camps, as an officer. He did not neglect his acquired skill at drawing and woodwork – the latter is an abiding interest. There were holidays with his family and an intense romantic relationship with a girl which had strong elements of bliss and agony alike.

The year 1951 was an important one. He received an offer from Professor Adrian to go to Sweden for six months to work with a distinguished scientist, Zotterman. It was an exciting opportunity for Habgood, but after some thought he declined. His mind was stirring in a different way.

As too often is the case in Habgood's type of conversion, it does not lead to a strong commitment to any particular Church. He usually attended Holy Trinity, where he eventually served on the Parochial Church Council. But it might as well have been Methodist or Congregational. He had little contact with religion at King's and never thought much of the Dean, Ivor Ramsay, whose response to any problem brought to him was, 'Have a glass of sherry'. Ramsay was miscast at King's, a tragic figure. On 21 January 1956 he went up onto the roof of the chapel and threw himself to his death from the West end.

Slowly Habgood was discovering the richness of the Church of England outside King's, Holy Trinity and his evangelical circles. He became attracted to St Benet's church, where he often went to pray. This church was staffed by the Franciscans and it was not long before Brother Michael (later to become Bishop Suffragan of St Germans 1979–85) had a real influence on Habgood. Another influence was the Vice-Principal of Westcott House, Harry Williams (now a well-known monk with the Community of the Resurrection, Mirfield) to whom Habgood was sent. They began with an argument about Charles Simeon after Williams had lent Habgood a book on Simeon and Church Order, but the conversation soon slipped beneath the surface to deeper things. Harry Williams was particularly good for Habgood. He had served in that Anglo-Catholic citadel, All Saints, Margaret Street, where vesture, gesture and incense were symbols, signs and smells of a dimension of life and worship hitherto unknown to Habgood.

The year 1951 was also the one in which Habgood voted Conservative in the General Election; and suffered greatly following the loss of life at a boys' camp in North Wales when a yacht was missing. But chiefly: '15 August. Visited Dean, told him of my desire to go into ministry.' Professor Matthews had high hopes for Habgood in another direction. As he wrote:

> The physiology laboratory was a world focus of research on the nervous system through the forties and fifties. The late Lord Adrian and his many collaborators made a breakthrough in applying electronic techniques to elucidate many problems of nerve function. The laboratory always had foreign visitors working in it, and was a mecca for free discussion of the puzzles of many very able intellects. A

> scientific career was wide open to John. However, I knew John well enough not to be surprised when he came to my room and simply said, 'Sir, I have decided to go into the Church.'

What had led up to this decision? Primarily Habgood had discovered people and secondly he had discovered the Church of England. Science could not fulfill his deepest needs.

Where should he undergo theological training? His older friends wanted him to go to an evangelical college for his training. His new friends suggested Cuddesdon and their judgement was right. In an interesting letter written to Major Batt, who was opposed to a Cuddesdon training, Habgood reveals the reasons for his choice:

> I suppose why I really want to go to Cuddesdon is because it offers two things: spiritual discipline and intellectual freedom. Spiritual discipline you may feel shy of, but remember that I am setting out on a life's work. It is not as though I shall have any other job or for one moment shall be able to escape from my spiritual responsibilities or difficulties: it is a frightening prospect. But surely you would agree that the most practical thing to do before any great task is to pray; it is not 'other worldly' to have a quiet time. I don't want to undergo two years of rigid spiritual discipline because I hope that the rest of my life is going to be modelled on what I did at college, but precisely because I imagine it is going to be very, very different!
>
> And then, intellectual freedom. Most colleges seem to concentrate rather on formal theology and the dreary business of passing exams. The policy at Cuddesdon seems to be that the exams don't really matter, but that it is important to read widely according to your own tastes. And that is just what I want.
>
> You see, some unbelievers doubt because they don't know what Christianity is; the remedy is simple and any reasonably competent knowledge of theology should suffice. But there are others who doubt even though they know what it is; I am surrounded by them, and they are the real challenge to me. I don't mean so much an evangelistic

challenge (though it may be my lot to work among such people when I am ordained), as a personal challenge to my own mental honesty: can I go through their experiences and read what they have read and find that through it all Christ shines as brightly as ever? A very deep thinker once wrote: 'I do not believe in Christ as a child, but my hosanna has come through a great furnace of doubt.' In a sense I must go through that furnace. I must not believe because I have shut myself up in a little watertight compartment filled with CSSM [Children's Special Service Mission] publications, but because I have myself explored every path. What I learn may be of no 'practical' value, but it will mean that I can be utterly sincere with the sincerity that springs from knowledge, not ignorance.

3

The Giddy Joke

Habgood's decision to be ordained, though final, was not made without qualms. Moving from the settled but stretching and stimulating milieu of King's College, Cambridge, where intellectual talk and scientific equipment were part of the staple food, to the theological slimline diet as a student at Cuddesdon, was not palatable. It cannot have been easy for a Cambridge Fellow who had recently collected a Ph.D to settle to a desert-like life without benefit of oasis. Cuddesdon was not a high point in Habgood's journey. Nevertheless, no hidden meaning should be sought from the fact that travelling on the train to his CACTM Selection Conference at Farnham Castle (before moving to Cuddesdon) Habgood read *The Possessed* and immediately afterwards read *Christian Doubt*. His arrival in 1953 was not helped by the change of Principal the previous year. Kenneth Riches had become Bishop Suffragan of Dorchester en route for the See of Lincoln. The new Principal was remarkably dissimilar: Edward Knapp-Fisher, later Bishop of Pretoria and Canon of Westminster Abbey. Each man left, even if he did not impose, a particular imprint on the life of the College.

Habgood may have pushed aside his CICCU outlook but he was depressed with the incredible churchiness of Cuddesdon. Surely this was not a microcosm of the Church priestly! He was quickly attracted to another newcomer who had a sparkling vitality about him. They became close friends. The fellow-student was Nicolas Stacey, a young naval officer, international athelete and later priest whose success and failure story was recorded in *Who Cares?*. It was the attraction of opposites in temperament, intellectual equipment and outlook. Each was to make a name in the Church of England in very different ways.

Nicolas Stacey writes:

> John was tall, thin, slightly stooping and quietly spoken with a shy, attractive smile. Although John and I are very different sorts of people I took to him at once . . . John, who has a quiet, rather dry sense of humour, was born wise and cautious. When I used to let off steam to him about all the things that irritated me at Cuddesdon, John was always calm, reasonable and self-disciplined. No doubt this was partly because he was a buttoned-up character who took himself and life very seriously but it was also because he had a maturity beyond his years. There are some ordinands and priests who, one always feels, would go to bed in their cassocks if left to themselves. John was not in this category, but I really never knew him to let his hair down. This may be partly because of his shyness.
>
> While I do not think he would claim to have great charisma or exceptional qualities of leadership, he has enormous integrity and a quiet purposefulness which, coupled with his outstanding intellect, made him a credible and respected figure in the College.

During long walks and talks Habgood would vigorously dissect and explain a lecture, squeezing more out of it than often it deserved. Stacey was full of energy, restless with plans for movements and causes. The possibility of starting a scheme of 'honorary uncles' for orphanage boys was just one of the projects explored. Habgood allowed his off-centre wit to concern itself with the Church of England Society for the Promotion of Interplanetary Travel or drafting an Application for Permission to be Ill for the Cuddesdon Health Service. Shortly before Ordination the two students went to hear Billy Graham at Harringay. 'Let's go forward and see what happens,' said Stacey. They did, and were counselled!

Sometimes guest speakers at the College were like beacons in the prevailing gloom. An example is noted in Habgood's diary:

> [1953] 13 May. Solemn Evensong – had to act as candle bearer – much to my rage. Final lecture by Mervyn Stockwood at 6.0 followed by very lively discussion till 9.29! At last someone who is prepared to face the situation as it really is.

It was a rare compliment. Habgood found the majority of preachers and speakers dull and unimaginative – reflected in a diary entry such as 'College sermon – rather like a devotional tract'. When Eric Mascall, then Lecturer in the Philosophy of Religion in Oxford University gave a talk, Habgood 'disagreed with practically everything he said'. Habgood's views were not kept to himself. Fellow-students included Philip Goodrich (now Bishop of Worcester), John Baker (now Bishop of Salisbury), Hewlett Thompson (now Bishop of Exeter) and Oliver Fiennes (now Dean of Lincoln). If they wanted to know what Habgood was thinking, they had only to turn to his articles on 'Sermons good and bad' in *The Spectator*; or, less likely, on 'Personality' in *Homes and Parents*, or 'A scientific approach to beauty.'

If Cuddesdon was disappointing, and perhaps he disappointed Cuddesdon, at least there was an opportunity for sustained reading. Although he probably knew more about the Bible than any other student (his CICCU experience had ensured that), the gathering enlightenment of modern biblical criticism was a new acquaintance although it was not pursued in detail. Greek had to be learned and church history offered a new vista of experience.

As for Habgood's future, it was hoped that he would be attached to the church of Holy Trinity, Prince Consort Road, Kensington, while acting as a chaplain to the University of London at Imperial College. It was to be a new venture using Habgood's scientific background in a scientific environment. The plans did not mature. Instead he went elsewhere in Kensington, joining a staff of six serving three churches: St Mary Abbots parish church; Christ Church, Victoria Road; and St George's, Campden Hill. He was made deacon in 1954 and ordained priest in 1955 by the Bishop of London (J. W. C. Wand) in St Paul's Cathedral. The vicar of Kensington, Stanley A. H. Eley, later Bishop of Gibraltar, was a good organizer and a strong critic. Much of Habgood's time was spent in preparing people, particularly adults, for confirmation and in house-to-house visiting. He was not like an ordinary 'pale-faced young curate', in view of his maturity in years and knowledge. Thus he was allowed much freedom; but the house-to-house visiting was compulsory, which proved to be good for him, curing strands of unsociability in his personality.

Unexpectedly Habgood had a rapport with children. He was good at telling stories and making the Bible a series of books to be enjoyed.

In view of Habgood's later thought and activity in the ecumenical sphere, it is important at this stage to record that his base was firmly Anglican. What he read and learned at Cuddesdon, practised at Kensington and pursued at Westcott House was the *via media* of Anglicanism, and an English version of it too. There is the story (not Habgood's) of the position of the Church of England being explained to a French lady. The usual phrase about Protestant and Catholic was mentioned. 'Mon Dieu!' exclaimed the lady, throwing hands and eyes to heaven. 'Protestante et catholique: c'est impossible!' And so it seems to many people. Habgood absorbed the teaching that if by 'protestant' one means non-papal and, by 'catholic' one implies a retention of the historic ministry, doctrine and sacraments, then the Anglican Church is as protestant as the protestants and more catholic than the Romans. He would not have argued with the question, 'Where was the Church of England before the Reformation?' and the counter-question, 'Where was your face before you washed it?' The Reformation in England was characteristically English in that it did not proceed by logically developing a theological or ecclesiastical system from some basic doctrine or position. It aimed at reforming the abuses in the continuing life of the existing Church.

Habgood seems to have been more deeply drawn to Anglicanism by admiring the Church's threefold emphasis on truth, freedom and development. Yet tradition has also been important to him. There are some Christian communions in which tradition exercises a dictatorship which deprives them of flexibility and renders them unaccommodating to any new ideas, even when the new idea is true. Again, there are other Christian bodies which attach to tradition only a very secondary importance; they disclaim all considerations of pedigree, and in consequence they seem to lack stability and sit loosely to old ideas, even when those old ideas are good.

Loyalty to the tradition has to be reconciled with the imperious and always unprecedented demands of experience. Here the tension! Loyalty to the tradition hardens into an unintelligent tenure of a formulated creed. Loyalty to the principle of progress degenerates into an easy surrender to the prevailing influences, political and intellectual, of the Church's secular environment. On the one hand, fanatical conservatism: on the other hand, licentious innovation. Between them there is the spectacle which history has offered of the Anglican Church carrying forward the old truth into intelligible and fruitful relation to ever-changing conditions.

In the mid-1950s such a Church had immense attraction to Habgood and it is easy to see why. It even appears to fit his personality. The *via media* is not an easy or straightforward way. Hooker warned us that things which seem plain may be more plain than true. Today the 'plain' way is more sought after than the middle way. The conflict of the two positions runs through the Church's record, its continuing scandal and its insoluble problem. Habgood is in the forefront with those who are seeking to discover some principle which shall both guarantee the integrity of the tradition and authenticate the process of indispensable change.

The ferment of the 1960s was still in the future. Now that Habgood was the other side of ordination, what did he think he was doing? What was the Church for? He saw the Church existing for worship, service and teaching, each having inward and outward aspects. '*Worship* may mean the specific activity of a body of Christians: or it may mean the more general sense of worth and significance which Christian insight can give to life in general. *Service* may mean love of the brethren; or it may mean the service of the world. *Teaching* may mean the building-up of the Body in the truth of Christ; or it may mean the proclamation of the Gospel to the world.'

Certainly the parson's functions appeared to be those of leading his people in worship, and offering on their behalf the praise and intercession they were unable or unwilling to give. In addition society still expected him to add a touch of respectability and easy comfort to the landmarks of life such as birth, marriage and death. The parson should be able to help his laity to show Christ to the world in the places where they live and work, but unfortunately in many cases his isolation from the world and also from his own parishioners' lives ends instead in a spiritually impotent pastor, left in charge of a decaying fabric, disguising his ineptitudes by devices that conceal a flight from reality.

How did Habgood face his future as a priest? An inferno-like Nicolas Stacey burns bright, gives off heat and uses all his energy in singular dedication. He wants success but may fail. He lives on the razor's edge with all the insecurity which such a position involves. It is the insecurity of an all-purpose activist.

There are other forms of insecurity. Habgood thought it important that any young priest should become a sort of intellectual and vocational Franciscan – intellectually and vocationally poor and with nowhere to lay his head, except in the ultimate security of God. This means both 'letting go' and opening up to a degree that Habgood found very difficult indeed. Although he did not know Fr H. H. Kelly (the founder of the Society of the Sacred Mission at Kelham), he was attracted to his thought, less to his way of life. Kelly was one of those men who trust God and have little time for religion. He would be an interesting figure in the Church today. Habgood once said to Westcott House students:

> One of the foundation principles of Kelham is a remark by Father Kelly: 'We have come here to serve God, and not to please ourselves.' If we are to think about Church and Ministry, this is where we must begin . . . Not with the Church nor with theological training nor with the changing structure of society. Some people get altogether too fussed about the Church. I think perhaps here we are in danger sometimes of indulging in orgies of ecclesiastical self-castigation . . . We get the whole thing upside-down if our first concern is the worthwhileness of the job as we see it now. If we once begin thinking like that it is a very little

> way to imagining that it is really rather splendid of us to be offering ourselves at all, that we are conferring some sort of favour on God, and we are wondering whether what he has for us is worthy of us. Unfair? Possibly – but – our vocation is rooted in the will of God. It is a gift from God, not a feeling. It is God's gift to the church through us.
>
> But – how do we know the will of God? 'Ah,' said Father Kelly, 'that's just the giddy joke. We never do.' Father Kelly wasn't a fool. He was putting in a paradoxical way what is a basic principle of the Christian life: absolute allegiance to the will of God. And the recognition that our apprehension of that will is always selective. There is an absolute and a relative aspect to the whole Christian faith.

Thus the will of God is not likely to be disclosed or understood through pious silences while on one's knees. It may be revealed in that way to those who are advanced in the spiritual life. To those starting out it is more likely to be discovered in the ministry they are given to undertake. Self-analysis is not particularly helpful when seeking God's will for oneself, neither is the lust for tokens and signs as evidence of divine guidance. People who hunger for these often refuse to recognize God's presence in what is normal, unexciting and commonplace. It it the very negation of the divine mind as disclosed in nature, in history, and supremely in the incarnation.

Kensington was no different from anywhere else. The Christian gospel was virtually irrelevant to the vast mass of people in the parish. Words such as God and love and sin and grace were already devalued. The pattern of society into which Christian devotion and churchgoing used to fit had been broken up. Religion was not even a pleasant and harmless appendage to life. It was an expendable irrelevancy to most people. In the mid-1950s the hardships of war had receded and the flavour of the 'better life', though not yet Macmillan's 'You've never had it so good', more easily grasped and realized in materialism, was both alluring and appetizing.

What was a newly ordained clergyman to do? What had he to offer? Habgood's experiences of some of his fellow-clergymen were not encouraging. In a contemporary essay he wrote:

> They present a picture of the Church as primarily an institution, a survival from a past era, which must somehow be 'kept going'. They have a basic feeling of insecurity which makes them bigoted; because they have lost the old sense of authority enjoyed by their forebears, because they have not the courage to let Christ vindicate himself, they shut themselves up in a little closed citadel of belief and put their trust in a system rather than in the living God. To many of those outside, the hollowness and inadequacy of their faith is only too apparent.

Such a picture was in Habgood's mind, and perhaps by keeping it in mind he was always saved from being drawn into the protective structures of the ecclesiastical organization. Similarly, he never suffered from drawing the distinction between authority and authoritarianism. Because of his consciousness of being under authority, he has always been able to exercise authority, albeit in a hesitatingly firm way which we will consider later in this study.

In retrospect his taste of parish life at Kensington was the best course for him. Going straight to a university chaplaincy as a priest adventurer may have been good for undergraduates but Habgood would have missed exposure to a wider world and experience of the fancies and foibles of parochial life. He would have missed something else too. By happy coincidence he was drawn into the circle of Mrs Owen, the widow of Leslie Owen, one time Bishop Suffragan of Jarrow and tragically briefly Bishop of Lincoln. A remarkable woman with critical antennae and spiritual depths, she attended St Mary Abbots and a badly conducted service or a poor sermon did not leave her silent. She was equally concerned for the inner life of priests.

The 'inner life' has to be more than a glib phrase for a priest. It must be the fount of inspiration and guidance for all outward activities. It may be what is most wrong with the Church at the present time, in that too many Christians are either trying to live the Christian life without any real inwardness of religion or are giving up the attempt because they find it cannot succeed without this.

This is not the place to probe Habgood's spiritual recesses, but a few points are worthy of mention. In giving spiritual counsel Habgood has always seen the need to involve professional counsellors, for example marriage, medical, psychological, as particular cases warrant. He also considers the Anglican reformers were wiser than some others in recognizing that confession before a priest is not simply dealing with a bad thing which has to be abolished, but a good thing which has gone wrong. 'In the Anglican tradition the priest is not a judge but a pastor: he is not there to assess sins, but to help sinners. This is why there is a lot of emphasis on giving counsel and quieting consciences. The priest is there to put our individual struggle in its proper context within the life of the Church . . . Confession means something to people who still believe that they have a lot to learn about themselves.'

Superficially it appears that Habgood's views on spirituality changed radically over the years. By the time he reached Queen's College, Birmingham, in 1967, he found a changed climate and a new expectation. By comparison his own outlook seemed dated, arid and unhelpful. There was a hunger for spirituality, and many people were looking to the East or even to drug-induced experiences for a spirituality with depth and meaning. In part these were illusory paths to walk or trip. There are no shortcuts.

Within the Churches there were very different starting-points, as shown by the accelerating popularity of such people as Anthony Bloom (who started with God) and Michel Quoist (who started with the world). And Habgood? Are there some constants? Kierkegaard taught him the value of *pausing*. A favourite and important quotation from Kierkegaard (who was talking about confession) was: 'What does it profit a man if he goes further and further, and it must be said of him he never stops going further; when it also must be said of him there was nothing that made him pause? For pausing is not sluggish repose. Pausing is also movement. It is the inward movement of the heart. To pause is to deepen oneself in inwardness. But merely to go further is to go straight in the direction of superficiality.'

Habgood knew the value of pausing in his earlier ministry, and finds it indispensable but more difficult now. The clamour for immediacy remains a characteristic of the age. It is a recipe for shallowness – 'a reed shaken by the wind'. When asked by clergy how they can prevent their minds from becoming closed and how they can prevent their inner lives from rusting, Habgood could well reply: 'Stop talking'. How sad to be the sort of person of whom it may be said, 'there was nothing that made him pause'.

Habgood told students at Westcott House and Queen's College not to conceptualize the truth but to contemplate it; pictures should come before plans; and God before religion. He was never one of the multitude who earned Tyrrel's condemnation: people who 'define a mystery, but have never felt one'. That is like trying to accept the cross without the wonder. Mystery and expectation go together and symbols cannot be far behind.

Habgood may not have liked some of the theological perceptions displayed by Eric Mascall but he thought Mascall had many good things to say about theological truths as mysteries. A theological image or picture or story is rather like a light shining aloft. We can see it though we cannot analyse it. There is a clear central area shading off into obscurity. Simplicity and images are important. Habgood remembers watching a nativity play at a special school at Christmas 1959: 'All the children were a long way below normal intelligence; most of them had idiotlike faces. The play itself was extremely simple and naive, and ended with a procession out to the stable where there was a living tableau. In the middle of it the man who was with me whispered; "It makes you see why the tradition took that form." I found myself almost in tears.'

At Christmas the doctrine of the incarnation is preached but the world concentrates on a picture and a story which win every time. They meet us at the level at which we really grasp truths by seeing them.

Habgood's quizzical penetrating eyes miss nothing even when they express little. But they are always alert and alive for surprises. C. S. Lewis may have been 'surprised by joy'. Unfortunately too few Christians are surprised by anything or anyone. One of Habgood's favourite passages from Francis Thompson's works conveys a belief in the surprisingness of the world. It is a childlike wonder.

> Know ye what it is to be a child? It is to be something very different from the man of today. It is to have a spirit yet streaming from the waters of baptism, it is to believe in love, to believe in loveliness, to believe in belief. It is to be so little that the elves can reach to whisper in your ear. It is to turn pumpkins into coaches, and mice into horses, lowness into loftiness and nothing into everything – for each child has his fairy godmother in his own soul. It is to live in a nutshell and count yourself king of the infinite space; it is
>
> To see the world in a grain of sand,
> Heaven in a wild flower,
> To hold infinity in the palm of your hand
> And Eternity in an hour.

Childlikeness is a quality which Christians can easily overrate. Some Christians are infantile. Childlike wonder is different from childlike vision. It means something precious and lasting. It is also vulnerable, quite different from simple faith which carries the seeds of gullibility. Childlike vision belongs to open minds, receptive ears and bright eyes. Simple faith is blotting-paper religion.

4

Is the Picnic Over?

This study is concerned with themes and movements of opinion with which Habgood has been or is concerned. Biographical asides are included only to give flesh to some of the subjects or to show a practical application of a theoretical theme. Habgood never remains in the university library, although his bookshelves show that he has never relaxed his reading and study.

In October 1956 Habgood left St Mary Abbots to return to Cambridge, this time as Vice-Principal of Westcott House Theological College. He succeeded a certain Robert Runcie who had been appointed Dean of Trinity Hall, Cambridge. The contrast between outgoing and incoming vice-principals is reflected in the words themselves – but more too! The Principal of Westcott House was Kenneth M. Carey, and he referred to the outgoing Runcie in these terms:

> During his time here as Chaplain and then Vice-Principal he has made quite a contribution to our life. It is not only that he has been an excellent teacher, not only that he has quickened our interest in all sorts of things outside the curriculum, nor that he has never let us forget the paramount importance of the parishes – all these things he has done supremely well. But I have never known anyone whom one so easily forgave for telling one's own funny stories – and telling them so much better; nor anyone who could enliven a staff meeting by such devastating and entirely unmalicious mimicry. And it goes without saying that we shall miss him most for his friendship.

Later, someone said that whereas Runcie was an enlivener Habgood was an enhancer.

Habgood remained at Westcott House for six years, years which were to see the Church of England rocked like a derelict on an uncharted sea. And Cambridge, more than anywhere else, was the focus of the ferment. It is necessary to mention only a few names to refresh the memory of that period – John Robinson, Alec Vidler, Hugh Montefiore, Harry Williams, Geoffrey Lampe, Howard Root, George Woods. To this list should be added Habgood's name. His chief value to the Cambridge atmosphere was in providing a different dimension, that of the gentle breeze rather than the chilling wind of science.

The results of the so-called New Theology were mingled. Some proponents were excavating theology while others appeared to be evacuating it. Nonetheless it permanently changed the climate in which future discussion and exploration would take place. One of the influential books of the period was *Soundings: Essays Concerning Christian Understanding* (1962) edited by A. R. Vidler with nine other contributors. Habgood's own essay, 'The uneasy truce between science and theology', received favourable comment. In reviewing this book, John Robinson, by then Bishop Suffragan of Woolwich, selected the essays of Howard Root (Fellow and Dean of Emmanuel College), Habgood, Harry Williams (Fellow and Dean of Trinity College) and Alec Vidler (Fellow and Dean of King's College) as the ones that went deepest. Of Habgood's title and essay he noted: 'This truce, however welcome at the moment to each side is, (Habgood) believes, dangerous for both. It is dangerous to theology because of the breakdown of communication it involves and because psychologically science is left in possession of all the field that seems to matter. It is dangerous for science because science becomes insulated from all concern for ultimate truth and degenerates into technology. "Theological answers must not be given to scientific questions. Yet there is not a totally unbridgeable gulf between the two disciplines; nor are scientists and theologians totally different kinds of people with no subject-matter or methods in common. We must keep the conversation going in the belief that in the long run those who care about science will make better theologians, and those who care about theology, better scientists." I suspect that this will be an article quoted quite a lot.'

Habgood spent much time defining terms. He did not make it easy for those who used the word 'science' without much thought. And theologians who were setting off bombshells all the time, whose explosive power was merely a loud noise, irritated him – and he irritated them. Those theologians who were plumbing the depths, taking soundings, were different. Habgood was never tired of explaining that the word 'science' is used to describe a system of knowledge, a method, and a power. In a lecture on 'The Effect of Science on Religion' he explained these three meanings.

> First, science can be thought of as a system of knowledge. Nowadays some basic scientific knowledge is shared by most educated people. Most of us take for granted certain ideas about the size and structure of the universe, ideas which had to be established by a long and difficult process of scientific discovery. In the same way, a growing number of people tend to see life in evolutionary perspective, and are learning to look at their fellow human beings in psychological depth. Much of this knowledge is superficial, and may even be misleading, but there is no need to argue the point that some scientific knowledge has percolated very widely. On the other hand, profound and detailed scientific knowledge belongs only to very few – perhaps in the last resort only to those who are doing research on a particular subject.
>
> The second use of the word 'science' is to describe a mood, an approach to knowledge, a way of evaluating evidence. Here the word means primarily 'scientific method', and although this is obviously closely related to scientific knowledge, it is not the same. There are many people with a smattering of scientific knowledge, who are extremely unscientific in their approach to knowledge. And there are others who may have very little scientific knowledge, but yet have a respect for evidence and a toughness of mind which shows that their approach to experience genuinely shares the spirit of science.
>
> The third use of the word 'science' concentrates mainly

> on the practical power which scientific discoveries have put into our hands. In this sense, it is 'science' which fights disease, builds bridges, moulds our culture through TV, and determines the ingredients of our toothpaste. It is the technological applications of science which have brought it home to the ordinary man, and made the power of science one of the greatest features of the modern world.

When 'science' is seen to embrace these meanings, it is very different from what one often sees caricatured. 'Give me facts', says the scientist, 'nice clear unambiguous facts unfolding in a beautiful logical order which nobody can dispute.' Such a figure is as dangerous as the theologian who says, 'Don't confuse me with facts, I've made up my mind.'

Habgood realized that any statement, whether religious or not, which claims to be factual, thereby puts itself within the orbit of science and must be judged accordingly. He is quick to distinguish between a scientific statement and an expression of an attitude. Thus he has been critical, even harsh, on science enthusiasts – those who have attempted to give popular expressions to their own views. It is as if he is fearful of enthusiasm, of presenting a case with enthusiastic conviction that both arrests attention and makes converts. Any hidden persuasion or pressure, any feeling of compulsion is always avoided. Thus of Teilhard de Chardin he writes: 'He gives the impression, rather, of being a sensitive, intelligent, and imaginative thinker, forced to thrash around in the circle of his own ideas, without the benefit of serious criticism, and hence without making real contact with either the science or the theology he cared about so deeply' (*Theology*. May 1967). Yet he made contact with people who go on admiring and studying his works, with even a Society to ensure that his thought abides!

In reviewing F. W. Dillistone's biography of Charles Raven, who combined meticulous scholarship with outstanding oratory, Habgood reveals more than respect – short of admiration – for Raven, but then draws back.

> The last time I met Charles Raven he strode up the stairs to my room, flung himself into an armchair, and apologized for being late on the grounds that he had had a mild heart

> attack that morning. Then, at the age of 78, he proceeded to hold a roomful of students spellbound for two hours while he expounded his favourite theme, the unity of science and religion. That was typical of the man – dramatic, electrifying, unforgettable. The eyes of a visionary, the voice of a prophet, the gestures of one totally absorbed, the seemingly effortless flow of language, the mastery of his subject which enabled him to deliver a major lecture or sermon without a note, these were the outward features which made him a legend in post-war Cambridge.
>
> . . . His numerous writings on science and religion will not, I believe, survive, not even the Gifford Lectures. I remember as a young graduate hearing him lecture on the evolution of the cuckoo as an example of the creative spirit at work, and feeling even then that there was something wrong. He never came to terms with the real strengths of mechanistic thinking in the so-called 'hard sciences'. Yet despite the blind spots, despite the fatal unwillingness to admit that truth might be dialectical, the man himself was a reconciliation. And this is why those who knew him loved him, and felt in him the power of God.

Raven was carried along partly by his own enthusiasm. There are many such people and Habgood worries about them because the enthusiasm begins to obscure and resist new enlightenment. Thus of Raven, Habgood wrote: ' . . . the new tide passed him by. Hoskyns was a threat; Barth an implacable enemy; post-war British philosophy a triviality. A critic once said of him: "He did not become the leader he might have been because of his utter inability to absorb or relate himself to a contrary idea." The preacher could not bear to be interrupted.'

The kind of scientist much admired by Habgood is one who combines impeccable credentials with an ability to write about difficult matters clearly and simply. There are too few of them, but one was P. B. Medawar whose book *The Art of the Soluble* (1967) Habgood reviewed for *Frontier*. The successful biologist is also witty and civilized. He plucks some of Medawar's sentences from the book, studies them and admires them. 'If politics is the art of the possible, research is surely the art of the soluble.' 'Today we realize that philosophers devise Systems because it gives them a nice warm comfortable feeling inside; it is something done primarily for their benefit, not for ours.' 'The Predicament of Man is at the stage now that people have sufficient leisure and are sufficiently well fed to contemplate it, and many a tidy literary reputation has been built upon exploiting it; anybody nowadays who dared to suggest that the plight of man might not be wholly desperate would get a sharp rap over the knuckles in any literary weekly.' It is more than pithy sentences which Habgood admires. Medawar conveys, in Habgood's words, the 'belief that the wise man spends his time tackling practical problems which he has some hope of solving; and, so far from being a narrowing activity, such a programme demands the best use of the creative imagination'.

Habgood's own style never reaches the scintillating heights of Medawar's. It is not that he is less confident but that he is more cautious. The words are there, the poetry is there, but there is a holding-back.

Any scientist needs the benefit of outside criticism. Equally the outside critic needs to appreciate a scientist's instinctive reactions to a problem. He also needs to be aware of an atmosphere or culture. Science has its faith, its church, its morals and its rituals. It is for many a deeply satisfying way of life, a cultural world inside which to find fulfilment. Habgood had witnessed this at King's College. It is a safe, enclosed world. Only when one emerges from the cool laboratory into the theological, clammy light of dawn do the questions and answers cease to be black and white. All is hazy. In *Science and the Renewal of Belief* Russell Stannard, a high-energy physicist and lay reader in the Church of England writes: 'An advantage of being a scientist is that this inclination to sit on the fence is not one to which we are particularly prone . . . Among the ranks of scientists are to be found atheists and Christians, but very few waverers in the middle.' In a review of the book Habgood retorted: 'Precisely. Straightforward questions must have clear answers. The essence of science is so to arrange experience that clear answers can be given. But what if life as it is actually lived does not, and cannot, have the same kind of clarity? And what if God has to be found as much in the fog of uncertainty as in the light of faith?'

Habgood tries not only to contrast science and religion but also to find common ground, to search for a synthesis. He is too tentative to be an innovator, but unbending enough to be respected. Religious, like scientific, concepts have at least three components of meaning: the empirical, the theoretical and the intuitive. He admitted that Harold K. Schilling's book *Science and Religion: An Interpretation of Two Communities* (1964) echoed almost exactly his own thoughts. 'The empirical comes direct from observational analysis; the theoretical is the result of trying to explain and correlate; and the intuitive refers to the basic givenness of what is being studied or the presuppositions involved in studying it,' writes Habgood. The intuitive is beginning to stir in Habgood. It is later to be seen in small groups and working parties and in some interesting reports. Following Schilling, he realized that 'positive reconciliation requires more than a philosophic *tour de force;* it must be felt and lived; it must be not only *thinkable* but *workable.*'

When Habgood pushes aside theological indecisiveness, it is the scientist at work. Scientific theories are not the ultimate expressions of truth, but they do have reliability. He is offended by inexactness and not easily lured by the subjective approach. That is why he was critical of John Robinson's *Honest to God.* It was presentation, not content, which irked him. Even reviewing Robinson's *Exploration into God* (*Theology* April 1968) he notes this time that Robinson 'has been far more careful in saying precisely what he means' but his outlook 'remains curiously individualistic'. Nevertheless he grants that Robinson 'produced an impressive restatement of Christian belief in God in terms of panentheism – the doctrine that God is in everything, but that his Being is not identical with everything. Theism, he claims, is only one of a number of possible ways of mapping that personal and ineffable reality we call God; and theism – at least in its popular forms – has ceased to ring any bells with the majority of western men, because it is too closely associated with a view of the world and an ontology which are discredited. Panentheism, by contrast, involves the acknowledgement of a claim, a mystery and a grace, meeting us through events and people at those points where life seems most real.'

However, the response to Robinson suggests he was communicating and, apart from *Honest to God*, in language that was both intelligible and provocative. In contrast, Habgood's early writings (though not substantial) suffered from their eirenic and civilized tone. They offered a careful and balanced treatment of the issue under scrutiny but paid the price of care and balance in not being 'easy reads'. They lacked converting power, and while being read and admired sometimes failed to convince. Drafting a chapter on 'The Language of Science' for a proposed (but unpublished) book on the language of religion sponsored by the British Council of Churches (1968–9), Habgood went far to defend scientific language.

> Any discipline which explores the frontiers of human knowledge must invent its own terminology; it must handle concepts which may have no counterpart in ordinary experience. But the enormous advantage of a vocabulary of technical terms is that the meaning given to words can be precise, and hence accessible to anybody who wants to learn, in contrast again to those other areas of discourse where meaning seems to get lost in a fog of verbal confusion. As for the dangers, the standard scientific answer is that it is better to know the truth than not to know it; and in any case, the responsibility for the way in which scientific discoveries are used does not rest with scientists alone.

'Language' and 'method' are intertwined. That is as true of science as of theology. Reference has already been made to Habgood's article 'The attractiveness of science' in which he gave a sympathetic account of the scientific attitude. In part it was a protest to theological outsiders who claimed that science is dull, difficult and dangerous; dull because it omits or undervalues the most characteristically personal, and hence the most interesting, aspects of human experience; difficult, because its findings are often couched in incomprehensible jargon; and dangerous, because, as every alarmist headline on the topic proclaims, it has unrivalled power to change, disrupt or even destroy our way of life. Habgood looked at scientific method and contrasted it with the method of theology. The points are important for any understanding of Habgood.

(1) Science is content to advance slowly, never allowing theory to run on too far ahead of fact. The speculativeness of much theology, often with only the feeblest anchorage in fact, compares very unfavourably with the gradual growth of scientific knowledge to the point at which we are daily prepared to stake our lives on it.

(2) The scientist always looks for the simplest explanation of a phenomenon and tries to present it in terms which can be strictly defined. Thus . . . 'love' is a word which can give rise to incalculable muddles, and the more one discusses it in terms of 'higher factors' the greater the muddle would seem to become. [Earlier in the article Habgood had pointed out that the proper way for a scientist to understand a phenomenon like falling in love is to analyse it into its separate constituents – physiological, sociological, psychological, economic, etc.] The scientist will always look for a 'reduced explanation' because he believes that that way lie clarity and agreement.

(3) One observer is as good as another. Hence the scientist has no need to concern himself with questions about authority, for the authority behind his statements rests solely on the fact that his results are repeatable.

(4) Scientific theories remain plastic. They are never proved in an absolute sense, but merely continue to evade disproof after continued testing. Thus they can always be expanded or modified to accommodate new facts, and the scientist's hope is that they will eventually accommodate all facts. Past experience has taught him that irregularities or apparently unique events can generally be found a place within the pattern, provided he is patient and not too ready to jump to premature conclusions about their uniqueness. There is a good example of this attitude in the British Medical Association's section of the report of the Archbishop's Commission on the *Church's Ministry of Healing* (1958). It is not denied that spontaneous remissions occur in certain diseases and that there are sometimes apparently

inexplicable cures. But it is quite a different matter to pass from this admission to talk about miracles.

In the late 1950s science seemed to be in an unassailable citadel. Ten years on, the pendulum was swinging with empty places in the science faculties of universities and government cautiousness (some say cynicism) was shown by the curtailment of grants for scientific projects. Science was in a corner and the leader writer in *Science Journal* (July 1968) asked the question:

> Is the picnic over? . . . There is a growing feeling that science alone is not the cure for all ills – particularly large ones – and that its indiscriminate use may even create more social problems than it solves . . . somehow the shortcomings, the failures, even the waste, had made greater public impact than the successes. Research still remains just about the most potentially profitable activity in which man can emerge. But for the next few years anyway the scientific community is going to have to prove this point and to prove further that science is applicable to humanity's most pressing problems.

Of course, people like Habgood had never seen science as a self-contained closed-circuit universe, yet ways had to be found to keep science pure while speeding its progress in a spotted world.

One book which had a great influence on Habgood was Michael Polanyi's *Personal Knowledge: Towards a Post-critical Philosophy* (1958). Polanyi came to have a considerable if controversial following but Habgood absorbed, admired and accepted *Personal Knowledge* almost as soon as it appeared. Polanyi was a physical chemist turned philosopher. R. A. Hodgkin puts his finger on the essence of Polanyi's philosophy in his entry for the *Dictionary of National Biography 1971–1980* when he writes:

> Polanyi, like his near-contemporaries F. A. Hayek and Sir Karl Popper, was trying to understand the relationship between freedom and orderliness, not only in the depths of nature but in the dynamic processes of human action and knowledge . . . (It) was the vision of a new kind of

> philosophy, one that would relate science harmoniously to other modes of human knowing, which drew him on.
>
> . . . Though Polanyi made full use of critical, empirical and analytical methods, he never gave them priority. He knew that the roots of science lay deeper and he claimed that the commitment of an explorer, or of a group of explorers, to the discovery of hidden order in the universe and of faith in that order were prior requirements for all acts of discovery. Empirical research and critical analysis follow. This reversal was the linchpin of his thought. It grew out of what he would have called his own 'tacit knowledge' for he knew it in his bones, from having done thirty years of successful, co-operative scientific research.' Thus, he challenged the conventional wisdom that scientists are cool and detached and that their judgements are value-free.

Habgood liked Polanyi's distinction between articulate and inarticulate knowledge and found it helpful. Habgood noted:

> Science is the great example of articulate knowledge. The aim of science is to describe and explain the natural world as clearly and accurately as possible, using words or symbols whose meanings are precise and whose relationships can be expressed as far as possible mathematically. This highly articulate body of knowledge is so impressive that some have claimed it to be the only reliable kind of knowledge there is.
>
> (However) such a body of knowledge may presuppose another type of knowledge, whose existence may go unrecognized – what Polanyi calls 'inarticulate knowledge'.
>
> To admit that there can be inarticulate knowledge clears away one of the basic theoretical objections to religion which is strongly felt nowadays. It allows us to believe that our gropings after the meaning of things and our sense of the mystery of existence are not simply mistakes and misunderstandings, to be removed by being a bit more scientific or applying the laws of logic more ruthlessly. It becomes possible to see how there can be a confused and partial knowledge of reality, which is genuine even though it cannot be brought within the bounds of science.

> Not all such claims to knowledge need to be taken with equal seriousness. The fact that knowledge is inarticulate does not put it beyond criticism. The history of any religion is in part the history of successive criticisms and refinements of its fundamental insights.

There are many ways of thinking about man's knowledge of the world and Polanyi as understood by Habgood opened up a particular one. Habgood writes:

> We know different facets of our experience in different ways and with different degrees of precision. There is a hierarchy of knowledge. At one end of the scale there is precise scientific knowledge of those features of experience which can be treated as objects existing independently of us; at the other end, there is the knowledge we have of other persons by our involvement with them, the kind of knowledge we can only have when we *stop* treating them as objects. At one end of the scale we have extreme articulateness, at the other end extreme inarticulateness. And just as there is an inverse relationship between articulateness and involvement, so there is also a relationship between involvement and interest. When we stop thinking about knowledge in the abstract, we have to admit that what interests us most is what involves us most as persons. Quite apart from every other consideration, a world of which we only had precise scientific knowledge would be appallingly dull.
>
> Paganism went wrong because it tried to come to terms with the world of objects through personal involvement; and it found gods in every bush. Scientific atheism went wrong, because it tried to reduce the whole of experience to our experience of objects. Agnosticism, I believe, goes wrong because it recognizes the limits of knowledge, but is too certain about precisely where those limits lie. Religiousness is always liable to go wrong either by claiming knowledge of a quasi-scientific kind, or by imagining that wherever there is a mystery, there is God.
>
> Religious knowledge belongs to the inarticulate end of the scale, and the kind of mystery which should concern it is therefore the mystery of our involvement with persons.

These paragraphs are taken from Habgood's first book, *Religion and Science.* Published in 1964, it was reissued in 1972 in a series of books 'for thinking laymen'. The series editor was Dr William Neil. The book was well received and its purpose achieved when it was used as a launching-pad to explore the subject further.

Habgood must have become rather tired with incessant requests to speak or preach on 'Science and Religion' in college chapel or conference hall, in parish pulpit or debating chamber. He was saved from the worst fear of single or specialist subject speakers, for each time a new speech or sermon was required it was written out in full. This ensured that repetitive themes were presented freshly.

Habgood contributed an essay to the *Expository Times* (January 1973) on 'They changed our thinking: Darwin and after'. He considers this essay as the best thing he has ever written. It did not pass without critical comment at the time and the controversy was reawakened by Hugh Montefiore, Bishop of Birmingham, when he reviewed *A Working Faith* (in which the essay was reprinted) in *Theology* (January 1981).

In the essay Habgood is dismissive of those who question Darwin's basic ideas, for he considers that these have been many times vindicated. 'In the last twenty (years), the molecular basis of evolutionary change has begun to be revealed and there are now no adequate scientific grounds for opposition.' He noted the differences between present-day evolutionary theory and early Darwinism: 'While not affecting the fundamental issues, some of these have changed the feel of the theory so that it seems less sharply antagonistic to belief in a loving Providence.'

Habgood mentioned five developments in evolutionary theory which added up to a shift of emphasis. They were:

> First and most important . . . the development of genetics and in particular the theory of mutations . . . Secondly, the emphasis in the theory has shifted away from the notion of the isolated individual locked in a life-and-death struggle against all other organisms, towards that of the population, or 'gene pool', as the evolving entity. Species, in other words, evolve as wholes. . . . Thirdly, one of the most

> powerful creative factors in evolution is seen to be environmental change . . . Fourthly, since Darwin's day it has become evident that behavioural change may be as important as structural change in ensuring the success of the species . . . A fifth development concerns the degree to which evolutionary concepts have been extended outside the realm of biological evolution.

Habgood closed his essay by asserting:

> In a universe which offers vast possibilities of choice, evolution by random variation and natural selection ensures that a wide variety of the possible modes of being should be explored. Teilhard de Chardin appositely used the word 'groping' 'It means pervading everything so as to try everything, and trying everything so as to find everything.' The profusion of life, the immense variety, the mistakes, the dead-ends and the failures all make sense on this view of things. Free creativeness drawing on an inexhaustible well of randomness is bound to lead to tragedy and waste and suffering. But it also seems to be the only possible basis for those higher levels of freedom in terms of which Christians have always defended God's wisdom in creation. The alternative, a universe planned in detail and unfolding inexorably as pre-ordained, containing no source of unpredictability within itself, would not only be intolerably dull but also unforgivably evil. Why should whole species be created only to be exterminated? Why should the apparent design of some parts of many organisms be so remarkably inefficient? Why death, unless its counterpart reproduction were essential as a generator of newness?
>
> I wrote earlier that I thought theologians ought gladly and gratefully to accept the full implications of Darwin's ideas. I am not the sort of enthusiast who claims that evolution is the gospel Christianity has always been waiting for. Nevertheless, I hope enough has been said to show that despite the difficulties this is a potentially valuable source of theological insight, and that no real alternative is thinkable, either scientifically or theologically.

Reviewing *A Working Faith* as a collection of essays, Hugh

Montefiore describes them as the result of 'a well-stocked scientific mind sharpened with theological acumen [Hugh Montefiore has a theological mind sharpened with scientific and technological insights], resulting in a sensitive and balanced judgement, with a grasp of ethical priorities elegantly and lucidly expressed'. After the bouquet, a missile.

> I find it hard to reconcile the sensitive moralist and theologian of two-thirds of this book with the hard-line, dogmatic scientist of the first part. The Bishop takes up Einstein's reaction: 'God does not play dice' but affirms that he does. He believes that the combination of random change and natural selection alone drives the engine of biological creativity. . . . It is high time that this central dogma of the natural sciences is no longer taken for granted. The case against it cannot, alas, be made out in a review, and so I must content myself with a mere quotation from one who has been a doughty fighter against scientific orthodoxy. Arthur Koestler wrote with good reason: "Darwinian selection no doubt plays a part in the evolutionary process, but only a subordinate part (comparable to the action of the selective weedkiller); and there is a growing realization that there must be other principles at work on the vast canvas of evolutionary phenomena.
>
> If neo-Darwinism is bad and outmoded scientific dogma, it leads to even worse theology. I cannot share the view that a process which is fundamentally based on chance can express the will of a loving Creator. All human experience of love points otherwise. Love is purposive. Love does not merely display itself: it reveals itself. And if God knows already the infinite implications of chance mutations, what pleasure can he take in setting in motion this random process so that eventually his fore-ordained purpose may emerge? What sort of providence is this? What kind of incarnation is possible? Teilhard de Chardin and Charles Raven are both criticized by the Bishop because they rejected strict neo-Darwinism. He simply *assumes* they were wrong. The case needs not assuming but arguing; and – as I see it – the argument swings in *their* favour.

This is the stuff of debate and the debate continues. It reveals two ways of looking at the universe and perhaps even of God.

5

The Threshold of Ethics

One thing that worries Habgood is the Church's seeming eagerness to proffer an immediate view or give a verdict on any particular moral problem placed before it. Instant comment rarely includes a word of wisdom.

The Church of England has too often been muddled in its thinking, confusing Christian ethics with moral theology. It has been stated that Christian ethics deals with general moral principles and moral theology deals with specific cases. In an article in *Theology* (December 1939) Professor M. N. Stewart noted the immense difference in atmosphere between the two. Moral theology breathes in and breathes out the Latin air with its legal overtones. Hence moral theology appears to have too much law in it, too much hair-splitting, too much deduction from first principles, too little attention to empirical evidence, too simple a notion of the term 'natural', and too little concern for perfection.

The big pre-war name in moral theology was Kenneth Kirk, Regius Professor of Moral and Pastoral Theology at Oxford (1933–7) whose influence carried forward during his years as Bishop of Oxford (1937–54). His reputation was unchallenged in his lifetime. Following almost in his footsteps was Robert Mortimer, Regius Professor (1944–9) and Bishop of Exeter (1949–73). Kirk's mantle fell to Mortimer, who was as rigorous a moral theologian as Kirk but he lived in a post-war world where the complexity of moral issues demanded a different approach. He gave expression to his anxiety about the new questions to be faced during a speech given at the Church Assembly on 4 July 1963:

The Church of England is beginning to pay the price for

> its neglect of, and even contempt for, moral theology during the last two or three hundred years. It is paying the price for an exaggerated exaltation of New Testament ethics at the expense of a Christian ethic which combines with the Gospel ethic the concept of a natural law. The great work of the schoolmen in reformulating the concept of the natural law as they found it in Aristotle and the making of it a basis and a support for the New Testament revealed ethic has been far too long ignored in Anglican circles. The result is that we have almost nobody within the ranks of Anglican theologians who is able to set out clearly and forcibly the concept of the natural law upon which, in fact, both Gospel ethics and ordinary sexual morality rest. [That referred to the matter under debate.] What is urgently needed throughout the whole of Christendom is a reformulation in modern terms of the concept of the natural law, taking into full account the assured conclusion of modern psychology. There is, indeed, here some room for hope because Roman Catholic moral theologians, both on the Continent of Europe and in the United States of America are already hard at work on this and the first fruits are beginning to appear in their publications. It is much to be hoped that the Anglican Communion will encourage its younger theologians to launch themselves out on to this field of theology, for until we have moral theologians capable of stating the moral law and the Christian ethic in clear and convincing terms, we shall not be able to rescue our people from this relativism and irresponsibility.

There were those in the Church who wanted to see a renaissance of Anglican moral theology. Current interest and controversy involved many people holding widely contrasting views. Some of the *Soundings* essayists represented a radical but untested view: Eric Mascall and his fellow Thomists a traditional and proven position; and the Bishop of Exeter pleading for a new grounding of Christian morality in the natural law. Could common ground be found? Was progress possible? One person who thought so was Gordon Dunstan, then a Minor Canon of Westminster and Secretary of the Joint Board of Studies (i.e. Boards of Education and Social

Responsibility of Church Assembly). Dunstan's considerable skills and gifts were undervalued, and perhaps underused, by a Church which is always suspicious of high intellect contained in a prickly shell. Subsequently he was F. D. Maurice Professor of Moral and Social Theology at King's College, London.

In September 1963 Dunstan invited a number of people to meet and discuss the subject, 'Christian Ethics and Natural Law'. A brilliant man, in personality the opposite of Dunstan, was asked to chair the meeting. He was Ian Ramsey, then Nolloth Professor of the Philosophy of the Christian Religion at Oriel College, Oxford. The other members of the group were G. B. Bentley, canon of Windsor; P. E. Coleman, chaplain to King's College, London and now Bishop Suffragan of Crediton; F. E. Le Grice, Sub-Dean of St Albans Cathedral, later Dean of Ripon; D. J. B. Hawkins, a Roman Catholic philosopher and parish priest of Godalming; R. F. Hobson, consultant psychiatrist at the Bethlem Royal and Maudsley Hospitals and Lecturer in Psychiatry, University of London, E. L. Mascall, Professor of Historical Theology at King's College, London; Dom Illtyd Trethowan OSB, of Downside Abbey; H. A. Williams, Fellow and Dean of Chapel at Trinity College, Cambridge; G. F. Woods, Fellow and Dean of Downing College, Cambridge, later Professor of Divinity at King's College, London; and Habgood, who was then Rector of St. John's, Jedburgh. Canon Hawkins died and his place was taken by the controversial Herbert McCabe OP, then of Blackfriars, Manchester, and subsequently Editor of *New Blackfriars*.

This was the first of many groups with which Habgood was to be associated. What was important about this one was that it dealt with foundations, and shaky foundations at that. Giving the inaugural lecture at the Ian Ramsey Centre at Oxford on 'Natural Law and Bioethics' (22 February 1985), Habgood referred to the group:

> There can be no easy appeal to simple moral rules in the face of complex new problems. There is a constant need for detailed empirical knowledge. Moral claims arise out of sensitive reflection on actual issues against a background

> of general moral commitment and insight derived from past experience, whether biblical or secular. At bottom, morality has to do with what is characteristically human and personal, and there is thus a kind of objectivity about it; it is more, much more, than conformity to the conventions of a particular society.
>
> These were the bare bones of our agreement. But about the degree to which rules are useful, and the kind of objectivity claimed, there were sharp differences.

Habgood never derides the classic moral tradition:

> We wholly misunderstand it if we think of it as a set of rules for slavish obedience. The essence of this tradition is that it centres on the search for the good life and the virtues needed to sustain it. It is thus open to the future, and open in the ways it is brought to bear on the actual complexities of life. There is no possibility of spelling out the good life in some formula from which appropriate behaviour can then be read off. The search for it is an essential part of living it. But the living of it in turn creates the kind of environment which makes the exercise of virtue possible. And in that kind of environment it is easier to see what ought to be done.

Here again we see Habgood acknowledging the validity of a traditional view at the same time as recognizing the need for a new radical dimension to be introduced. At the very first residential meeting of the group positions were being taken up with Mascall and Williams at the outer edges and then all shades moving towards the centre. With some there was the assumption that there is a moral code based on revelation which Christians want to commend, or for which at least they seek for common ground 'outside'. Another view was that believers and unbelievers, caught up in life together, could do no more than work out the best mode of life together. For Habgood the distinction was too sharp. Christian morality has always been a comment on ordinary natural morality – taking up pre-existing patterns of human behaviour, such as the family. Attempts to justify these views in exclusively Christian terms do not carry conviction; there has always been a dialogue between the 'within' and the 'without' of the Christian tradition. As Habgood said, 'We are trying, not to commend answers which we have, but to discover them – in belief as in morals.' Harry Williams saw the believer and unbeliever in every man. Eric Mascall could not persuade people that they were really Christians when they denied it. This was a strange contrast, for Mascall's view appears more honest and more respectful of persons.

The greatest syllabus of Christian ethics is not a moral treatise, but a hymn to charity. The flavour of morality depends on its motive and sanction. It is at this point that the Christian departs from the Jewish moral code, for love rather than legalistic obedience undergirds Christian moral law. We are back to Williams, and still Habgood is both drawing from and sending down the well his particular contribution. The interplay of minds and subject-matter in the group led to some interesting papers, many of them published in *Theology*. The book that was at first planned never materialized. From Habgood there are papers on 'Moral Discovery' (*Theology*, June 1966); 'Faith and Forgiveness' (*Theology*, September 1960); 'Censorship' (*Theology*, September 1966); 'Filial responsibility'; and 'Is ethics a science or an art?'

The topics varied but the approach was the same. Gone were the hardened certainties and not yet come the instant enlightenment – as many people thought. 'Situation ethics' was gaining adherents with its trinitarian mode of love, freedom and spontaneity. Joseph Fletcher argued that love only was always good and the situation rather than the rule was the guide. Habgood thought it 'superficially attractive' but more superficial than attractive.

The new and sounder approach to moral reasoning embodied adequate knowledge of the empirical facts and a reliable styling of the Christian vision. The big question remained: Does Christian ethics have a distinctive content? That is not the case if one is looking for distinctive rules. Distinctive and permanently valid attitudes deriving from a distinctive and permanently valid example are a different matter. In this context words such as love, joy, peace, long-suffering, mean something.

Habgood found three different notes to specify the Christian approach to morality.

Hope, Heroic Faith and Receptivity. These are very nearly, but not quite, the traditional theological virtues Faith, Hope and Agapé. Some change of emphasis seems to be desirable since Faith and Agapé have been partly taken over by secular humanism and my aim is to draw out the special features which would seem to belong to a religious morality alone.

1 Hope is the only one of the three which can be left unchanged, because it has always been seen to belong in a peculiar way to a religious outlook in life. Only a religious basis for morality can give us grounds for hope. I do not mean 'pie in the sky when we die'. I mean the feeling that there is an ultimate worth and significance in the moral life. In contrast to the secular humanist, to hope is to assert that our values are not simply created by ourselves. In relation to other people, in relation to the world situation in which we find ourselves, we are to be creative and adventurous. But in relation to God, creation is a form of discovery. Thus the Christian hope is that we are not simply building castles in the air, but that there is an abiding reality which makes sense of all our efforts. In relation to love, hope adds the dimension of eternity which gives love its real depth; it assures us that what we know of love now is only a foretaste; it allows us to give full value to that element in love which is always looking for more. 'Now we see through a glass darkly, but then face to face.'

2 Closely linked with it is heroic faith. I call it 'heroic' faith, because everybody lives by faith of some kind. The word 'heroic' is intended to suggest the 'how much more' element in Christian living. It has been called 'the doctrine of the second mile'. Sometimes it shows itself in heroic sacrifice, sometimes in heroic obedience. It is the quality which derives from spiritual vision; the ability to see another person, not merely as one more human being, but as somebody worth treating with a selfless regard because he matters to God. It is spiritual vision, the fact that we can dimly grasp the infinite possibilities of another person

> in relation to God, which gives Christian concern its special quality.
>
> 3 Receptivity. This is the word especially used by Professor Donald Mackinnon [in *A Study in Ethical Theory*]. By it he seems to mean the sort of reverence and humility that should go with a religious outlook on life; the sense of mystery and dignity that should surround our relationship with other people; the quality of inwardness which is lacking in those who are always judging morality by its outward effects rather than by its effects on the soul. The receptive man is the man who cares about facts, who is not going to be content with snap judgements or slick formulae, but is deeply conscious of the complexity of the moral choices that we actually have to make. He is aware too that we are sinners in a sinful world so that even the highest that men can do is not enough.

This is 'pure Habgood'. He is not saying that hope, heroic faith and receptivity are the entire content of Christian morality,

> but against the background of modern western civilization these seem to sum up the distinctive flavour that the actively Christian approach to morality should give. It need hardly be added that the flavour is not always very strong. In the Church we find everything from a stuffy, finicking legalism to a benevolent indulgence. It cannot be said that the main impression conveyed by the Church's ethical thinking is that the basis of it is a creative personal relationship showing itself in a courageous and hopeful acceptance of new responsibilities. Probably the main impression given is that Christian morality is negative and dull, an impression powerfully reinforced by looking at almost any form of self-examination in some of those terrible little books of personal devotion (*Church Quarterly Review*, October–December 1963).

Taking one issue, that of censorship, it is interesting to see how Habgood applies his views. As a fact-gatherer he is exemplary. He see the facts in their just proportions and discerns tendencies as well as situations. This is the scientist.

What he discloses he interprets. This is the moralist. What he interprets he neither exalts nor condemns. This is Habgood. It is at this point that some people get annoyed with him – those who want to be fed with instant snacks from spiritual take-aways! Yet he is not an impersonal reflector, but an interpreter of the depth of moral issues, penetrating because sympathetic. Censorship is a subject on which people take sides. At first glance the conflict of opinions is irreconcilable.

Habgood does not stand outside and make his point from there. He is at the centre shaking his sieve, sorting the wheat from the chaff. He is not much concerned with the bigots at the extremities. They have corrupted themselves by expelling reason from their minds.

Censorship is one of a society's methods of protecting what it holds to be sacred. This definition applies pre-eminently to religion, but also by analogy to royalty, sex and violence. Sacredness can be interpreted very loosely to include all that depends on an element of mystique or on the validity of certain symbols to retain its value.

Habgood's paper on censorship was one of the working papers for the Christian Ethics and Natural Law group. In it he argued that while objects of reverence can in general look after themselves, the symbols through which their sacredness is conveyed to us are more vulnerable.

> Reverence is a profound human emotion of great personal and social importance. The fact that it can often lead to blindness and hypocrisy is a reminder that it is possible to be stupidly reverent about the wrong things; but to do without reverence at all is to be lacking in human depth. The key question concerning censorship is whether it can safeguard the kind of social conditions which allow the genuine expression of reverence, while making it possible to expose humbug.
>
> Its opponents argue that humbug can only be exposed when even the most sacred mysteries are open to attack. Nothing really valuable can be destroyed, because if anything succumbs to the attack and fails to shine by its

own light, it cannot have been all that valuable in the first place.

Up to a point this is true. God does not need our protection; blasphemy does not affect him. Our national leaders can stand a certain amount of mockery, because in the last resort they hold the power. Sex goes on pointing beyond itself, however much it may be cheapened. Human beings can have a dignity in suffering, however much it may be denied.

But while the blasphemer does not destroy God, he may blunt his own ability to respond to God; if he goes on to commit sacrilege, he may do the same for others. Unbridled mockery of royalty and of national leaders does not destroy the sovereign power of the state; but it may destroy some of the mystique surrounding the notion of sovereignty, and force those in power to wield it in a blunter and less permissive fashion. The dissipation of any sense of reverence for sex does not provide immunity from its ability to disturb us at a deep level; but such disturbances may cease to have any moral or creative value. Human life remains sacred, even in a concentration camp, but it may be infinitely harder to think of it as such.

In a confused society censorship can inhibit serious and legitimate criticism; arouse the desire for what is forbidden; and discriminate unfairly between different beliefs about what is sacred. As there is nothing censorious in Habgood's character, so he shrinks from censorship. He has said, 'There is a potential censor in each of us, wanting to lord it over others'. But in the end he recognizes that some censorship is necessary.

As with censorship, so with other moral issues. Habgood regards human beings as reasonable beings. Nevertheless man's self-awareness depends on his acceptance of some taboos, that is, some degree of social conformity.

Habgood holds that Christian ethical insight is fundamentally a theological insight which alters the Christian appreciation of the facts. In a 1970 book review he wrote: 'Christians differ from non-Christians in their moral judgements not usually because they accept different imperatives, but because they see the world in different ways; the differences, in other words, are theological.'

For Habgood ethical principles and practical issues stemming from them cannot be separated or untangled from the theology of creation and the question of 'newness' which is in Christ. This may sound innocuous or woolly but it cannot and must not be avoided. After all, Christ is the clue to creation. It was a subject considered by Habgood in his contribution, 'The theology of creation', to a volume entitled *Christianity and Change* (SPCK 1971). He asked questions about the nature of the gospel. In what sense was Christ new? In what sense did he fulfil the Old Testament; or destroy it; or transform it? He asserted that 'the newness of Christ himself, as "the agent of all creation", must somehow be the paradigm in terms of which all newness is to be understood'. It was a constant theme at this period. The key question was the relationship between old and new; his thinking was in terms of the creative process rather than of some unimaginable original act at the beginning of time. Thus he could write:

> If we hold that creation is essentially something mysterious and disruptive, if our main understanding of Christ is that he breaks in and shatters all that went before him, then presumably we shall be pentecostalists or revolutionaries. We shall not be afraid of the loss of the old, because for us it is incomparably less than the glory of the new. If, on the other hand, we see creation as a delicate process of building up complex structures, physical, social, mental, within which the new can emerge, if our main understanding of Christ is that he gave a new meaning to the tradition to which he belonged by transforming and expanding it, then presumably we shall be conservative reformers. I know this is a grossly over-simplified contrast. But it illustrates the kind of connection worth looking for between our theological and philosophical thinking on a subject like creation, and those attitudes of mind and value judgements which determine how we actually react to the startling novelties of our world.

Here Habgood positions himself, for he is certainly no revolutionary or pentecostalist. He is wary of the former and shudders at the latter. Somehow each seems to sit light to reason and veracity. The 'conservative reformer' is nearer the mark, but even that is not a neat or an exact description. His own innate cautiousness – and it is usually cautiousness not tentativeness – is controlled but deceptive. Many of his spoken and written words have a diluted feel about them, as if something has been drained from them. The radical essence which is a strong element in the mixture comes out as liquid reformist. Is this because he is neither manipulative nor dogmatic? He may be sure that he is right on this or that particular subject but normally he holds back from 'pronouncing'. When he does, his critics accuse him of being arrogant.

The revolutionary and pentecostalist are dismissed but not the rebel and non-conformist whom he regards as an essential member of society. In his first major public address, to the 73rd Congress of The Royal Society of Health meeting in Blackpool during April 1966, he said:

> The rebel and non-conformist are the perpetual reminder that the conformities within which most people live can become a prison depriving them of the fullness of life which might be theirs. The Danish philosopher Kierkegaard was tormented all his life by the problem of how to be a Christian in Christendom; if to be a Christian is to set out on a radical adventure of faith, how can this be done in a society where everybody regards Christianity as the most normal and natural thing in the world? This is the same problem translated into religious terms.
>
> Kierkegaard himself raises a further problem. He . . . was a depressive. Psychologically he was a deeply disturbed and unbalanced person, whose disturbance acted as the driving force of his creative genius. There are hundreds of similar examples: Kant, Beethoven and Blake spring at once to mind. The Saints provide a peculiarly rich field for the investigation of oddities. St Francis, St Teresa, St Joan, even St Paul might have found themselves today in a psychiatrist's consulting room. St Catherine of Genoa suffered acute mental and physical symptoms, probably hysterical, yet she was one of the great mystics and her life has formed the basis for one of the most comprehensive

> studies of mysticism. All these were people who have enriched human life, and altered the course of history, and whose abnormalities cannot be dismissed as unfortunate incidentals. By going to the very brink of human tolerance in creative achievement or mystic insight, they overstepped the bounds of what is normally called health.

Here is the difference. The revolutionary and pentecostalist mouth the word freedom but their concern is power. The rebel and non-conformist are true liberators opening up new vistas.

Habgood is not concerned with power. It is one reason why he changed his views on Teilhard de Chardin. In 1960 he was effusive in describing *The Phenomenon of Man* as 'a great work'. In subsequent years he concentrated on the worthwhileness of exploring the spirit and vision of Teilhard while being somewhat dismissive of his synthesis. He considered that Teilhard started as a visionary who saw the immense potentialities of man with science as his instrument, and ended as a prophet of inevitable progress, more and more obsessed with human power. He expressed this at a private conference on 'Science and Human Potentiality' at St George's House, Windsor in 1967. He said that Teilhard was fundamentally right in interpreting the world with man as its centre and standard of reference:

> We cannot in the end escape from some refined form of anthropocentricity if we are 'to make room for thought in the world', to do justice to the unique phenomenon by which alone the cosmos has come to some understanding of itself.
>
> The point is a philosophical one, more than a scientific one, though Teilhard gave it a scientific dress and marshalled a lot of evidence to show how in practice it is neglected and ignored by many scientific interpreters.
>
> But, granted that human consciousness should be of central importance in our interpretation of the universe, granted the reality of human power, it doesn't follow that the pursuit of this power can be elevated into a quasi-religious duty:

> The dream which human research obscurely fosters is fundamentally that of mastering . . . the ultimate energy of which all other energies are merely servants; and this by grasping the very mainspring of evolution, seizing the tiller of the world . . . I salute those who have the courage to admit that their hopes extend that far; they are at the pinnacle of mankind; and I would say to them that there is less difference than people think between research and adoration.

Note how the 'seizing of the tiller of the world' inevitably becomes the prerogative of the élite. Power, here, has become an end in itself. Theology has become so transformed as to be unrecognizable.

How Habgood deals with the realities of ethics and power will be considered later in this book.

6

Touching and Passing By

In 1961 Kenneth Carey left Westcott House to be Bishop of Edinburgh. In him one found a sane spirituality and a realistic radicalism. He was ever wary of counterfeit sanctity, of theological colleges turning out a bunch of sanctimonious Holy Joes. He once wrote that the colleges should produce men, 'who are eager to sacrifice, suffer and serve'. The priest should be in some sense a balance of saint, sage and seer. Carey had these ingredients in his trained character and disciplined life. He influenced Habgood in all kinds of unexpected ways. Some of his views made Habgood rethink a prepared position. For example, Carey put his finger on a possible theological weakness in the Parish Communion movement where there seemed to be an overemphasis on 'fellowship' and 'offering' and insufficient stress on what is received or, rather, whom we receive in Holy Communion. It was a view Habgood came to share without its undermining his support for Parish Communion.

Carey had not finished with Habgood. Within six months of Carey's moving to Edinburgh, Habgood was invited to be Rector of St John's, Jedburgh, in that diocese – although he was not instituted until 19 September 1962. His five years at Jedburgh coincided with a period in the Church of theological exploration, liturgical adventure and administrative reform. Movements and organizations galore failed to entice Habgood into their lairs. While accepting and promoting the ideas of particular societies he joined few of them. He enjoys being a collaborator in the realm of ideas rather than an avid planner with a programme and a platform of reform. Yet he lost no time in moving the Church along a radical road at Jedburgh. It sounds tame by current standards but it was not so in the early 1960s. Experiments came quickly and continuously. A congregational meeting was established as the forum where people could think together as a Church; the Eucharist was rediscovered by making some fundamental changes to its shape; public rather than private baptisms were encouraged; the worldwide Church received much attention and a focus when St John's paid for a student from Ghana to come to Edinburgh; tea-parties were 'out' and house meetings were 'in' where serious subjects were studied; the Christian churches in Jedburgh met to discuss and face hard topics, such as the meaning of Holy Communion, rather than rest content in occasional united acts of witness; members of St John's were encouraged to invite children from the slums of Glasgow to spend a holiday with them. 'Science and Religion' was a constant theme though never an obsession. There were many radio broadcasts too. These were just a few of the changes and chances at Jedburgh. There was nothing exceptional about them. They were happening all over England, though perhaps less so in Scotland.

In Jedburgh we see Habgood beyond the Westcott House theories of the ordained ministry or the testing of his calling at St Mary Abbots, Kensington. For the first time he had a cure of souls. It is interesting to see him at work in Scotland where the Episcopal Church is not the established Church. He was the priest to the gathered congregation rather than the parson of the parish. This may have limited the possibilities of uninvited contact but it does not seem to have diminished his view as to the work of a parish priest.

A major theme of his ministry and his teaching on the priesthood is that of 'touching and passing by'. While accepting that any parish priest wants to see a church full of disciples, a band of committed men and women, there are more frequently people who come and go. There are numerous casual contacts in the daily life of any priest. What does or should he do? Try to make a personal impact? Endeavour to display his personality? One cannot imagine Habgood doing that – certainly not overtly. In isolating two aspects of the ordained ministry he reveals something of himself. In many talks and lectures he refers to priests as 'outposts of eternity'. That is only possible through prayer, and prayer is a great focus, force and steadying influence. 'We cannot bring people to Christ if we ourselves are perpetually jangled, fussed, rushing here and there, starting this new scheme or that.' If he finds himself slipping away from this view he remembers his days in Kensington. His landlady kept over her mantelpiece a framed picture with the single word 'Eternity' on it. He recalls: 'It was the focus of the room, as it was the focus of her life. And I have never ceased to be grateful for the experience of living with someone who knew and was living in eternity, whose mind and heart had ascended with the ascended Christ.'

Habgood also stresses that 'a priest must have the quality of impersonality . . . This is a hard saying and it can easily be taken in the wrong sense. It does not mean that our personality is a thing of no value. But when we look at the Gospels it is difficult to think of our Lord as primarily "a personality". In fact his personality was quite extraordinarily elusive. What people seem to have been most conscious of in meeting him was not primarily a personality, but a mystery.'

Habgood remembers a woman in a Northern industrial parish talking about a curate, a charming young man and a hard worker. She said: 'The trouble is that he's not the sort of man you can tell your troubles to because he feels them so much that you don't like to add to his burden.'

The remark struck Habgood with force. Here was a young priest loving his people, sympathizing deeply with them, entering into their problems yet failing to do the very thing he was ordained to do because he was failing to point them away from himself to Christ. As Habgood noted, 'He had become a personal friend to all his people with all the limitations of human friendship'.

Is not this what causes priests to break down, suffer from ulcers and wavery perspectives? A priest can bear, in a sort of way, the sins and sorrows of a few friends: he cannot do it for a parish.

> It is Christ who bears the sins of the world, not we; it is his sympathy and love and presence which transforms the situations, not ours; and one of our tasks is to take the sin and the misery, the burdens that weigh down other people

> and put them on Christ who meets them. When we talk about identifying ourselves with other people it is Christ who must go out from us, who has already identified himself utterly with them. When we talk about the gap to be bridged, he is the bridge.

It is clear from Habgood's writings that he thinks the Church of England is confused about the ordained ministry. The difficulty starts with the Church's slipshod thinking on the diaconate. Once the deacon becomes a priest it is as if his diaconate is shed like discarded skin, reminding one of snakes which slip easily out of and away from their old scaly covering. It is a mistaken view. A priest is always a deacon, as Habgood had occasion to remind the General Synod in a debate on The Deaconess Order (12 November 1981): 'The diaconate is a lifelong ministry. Half the people in this chamber are members of it. This is not a sophistical point but an extremely important theological point, that the diaconate is and remains a theological and sacramental reality.' Why? He answered this on another occasion: 'It is not easy to be a symbolic person, to symbolize servanthood in a world where status and prestige and independence are among the most desirable goals. To be a servant – a deacon – is to be at everybody's beck and call. To be ordained is to be marked out as one who is available. It is to be made vulnerable.'

The word 'servant' is dangerously overused. It can become the cant of the patron under the guise of 'serving others'. On the lips of certain Christians it can be dangerous. Preaching in Great St Mary's, Cambridge (26 May 1968), Habgood presented the paradox and pointed the danger.

> If one of the temptations of service is patronage, then another is 'God-almightiness'. 'We ought to serve God rather than men' is one of the great charters of freedom in the New Testament. It was this which gave the early Church courage to cut loose from the conventions of its day, to defy public opinion, to survive centuries of persecution. The belief that they were on God's side, and that God must conquer, has created saints and martyrs – and inquisitors and pompous vicars. There's the difficulty. To speak in the name of God, to believe in the power of

> God, can not only give a man great courage and freedom; it can also blind him and make him inhumane. And the same is true in other contexts. The servants of humanity can become so obsessed with their own ideas and plans, their visions for the future, that in the end they destroy the humanity they intended to serve.

Once in the late 1950s when Habgood was in a muddle, he wrote in the front of his Bible the words 'Lovest thou me? Feed my sheep'. Years later he said: 'I still believe that in the last resort this is the only question for a Christian that ultimately matters: Lovest thou me? and for a priest this is the only command which he dare not disobey. "Feed my sheep!" The Gospel is reduced to barest simplicity in that moment of almost breathless calm before the disciples are once again sent out into the ordinary hubbub of life.'

These views may lighten the darkness but they do not appear to brighten life. There is something austere and intense about them. It is understandable if one appreciates that a priest is there to lead people from death to life. The ordinary life of the Church is mostly about trivialities, but at the heart there must be seriousness, and it is best if it is relaxed seriousness. To believe in God is to believe that there *is* a still centre to life, a hub to the wheel. So much for God – who can look after himself. The problem is the Church, which constantly obscures the gospel by fussing about the wrong things; by being trapped in the past; by making incredible claims to be the body through which God works, and by failing so miserably to live up to them.

Nonetheless it is within this body that the priest ministers. Habgood places stress on the priest as teacher, preacher and moral adviser, although he would be nervous of using the words 'moral adviser'. As teacher, Habgood means more than one who imparts knowledge. When he arrived in Jedburgh he was greeted with the remark, 'Rector, you tell us what to do and we will do it.' Apart from shuddering at the thought of this expectation of paternalistic leadership Habgood knew that one of his primary tasks was to look for buried treasure, in the lives of those among whom he ministered. Preaching at an institution in the Durham diocese in 1975, he said: 'A teacher doesn't stuff information into people. He tries to help them discover what they can do. He encourages, he corrects, he stimulates, he enables. An enabler helps you to discover yourself.'

Many people in the pews prefer a blackboard-and-chalk approach to teaching, with even the threat of the swish of a spiritual cane to aid their concentration and absorption. However, this suggests a passive laity who do as they are told, learn as they are taught and follow where they are led with little or no initiative of their own. This may be comfortable for both parties in some ways, but it often leads to an overstrained clergy who feel threatened by lay initiatives and yet long for the help they are unable to accept. Unfortunately, by relying on the odious side of paternalism – 'teacher knows best' – many a man has used the ordained ministry as a means of self-assurance. He has in fact substituted being a priest for being himself. The person is supposed to be the servant of the ministry and not the ministry the servant of the person.

Habgood turns the teaching office on its head. In place of a paternalistic and authoritarian ministry comes a sharing one. Priests who share their ministry with lay people are better able to understand the nature, strictures and processes of society and the meaning of the omnipresent secular. Many of them are naive about institutions and social structures. They can be naive about the nature and use of power; they are afraid of it and yet they often grab it and use it unwisely. This fear of and lust for power correlates with the matter of authority. Many want authority for themselves but resent being under authority and are, therefore, unable to exercise it when appropriate. Authority is not authoritarianism, as we shall see when Habgood becomes a bishop.

One begins to see a radical appraisal of ministry emerging in Habgood's approach to ministry. In the gathered organizational church the priest is the chief minister and the laity assist as teachers, officials, and so on. In the dispersed church, the laity, immersed as they are in the secular world, are the chief ministers and the clergy should assist them as resources, which means clergy should be more highly trained *theologically*.

There is no doubt that sheep who look up to be fed with

pre-digested food by Habgood are disappointed. They are sent empty away. He has endless patience in exploring and explaining particular points of theology or other subjects with students or congregations but they must engage their minds and wills. Sometimes he overestimates the intelligence of his audience (for he would not want to 'talk down' to people). As a part-time lecturer at Edinburgh Theological College during his Jedburgh years he failed to appreciate that the general level of intellectual attainment of the students did not equal that of students at Westcott House. His lectures, though brilliant, often sailed above the heads of many students.

The preacher is different. Habgood has gained a reputation as a thoughtful and stimulating rather than a forceful preacher. Endless pains are taken over sermons which are written out in full and usually at a single sitting. One might have expected him to fight shy of a form of communication which smacks of authoritarianism. The image of the parson in the pulpit as 'six feet above contradiction' is hard to dispel. But Habgood has always regarded preaching as part of worship. The worship is essential to it. It ought to flow out of worship and lead back into worship. Yet there is a proper authoritative aspect of preaching which no preacher can deny. In an introductory essay to *Queen's Sermons* (1977) Habgood covers the point in this way:

> . . . Anyone who feels called to preach at all must have seen some truth which he longs to share. There is a difference between conviction and dogmatism. There is a difference between having seen some truth, and claiming to speak in the name of all truth. There is a difference between knowing what we believe and refusing to respect the beliefs and experiences of others. And these differences are essential for the preacher. He must speak with a humble authority as one who knows, and yet knows above all the limitations of his knowledge. As he speaks out of learned ignorance his very limitations will reveal something of the dimensions of the truth he is seeking to convey. His authority is not that of the wise man and the scholar, important though wisdom and scholarship may be, but that of a lover who must

> express his delight in what he loves even though he has scarcely begun to glimpse its full extent.

In the same essay he mentions the personal involvement of the preacher in his subject. Preaching has been described as 'the communication of truth through personality.' This does not mean that the preacher should project himself with dynamic force, become a 'personality'. After all, he is merely God's blunt instrument. It does mean, in Habgood's words, that 'out of a curious amalgam between what the preacher is, how he prays, his experience, his aliveness to the world, his relationship to the congregation, the depth of his conviction, there can occur an event, a meeting with God'. No preacher should underrate his capacity to be used by God and Habgood is no exception. He may not 'let go' into uncontrolled acceleration but his steadiness on the spiritual road allows the Holy Spirit to move freely without recourse to using the safety belts. Forcing the spirit, as some preachers do, must surely be wrong and dangerous, even faithless.

On many occasions Habgood refers to the primary aim of preaching as being to arouse, strengthen and deepen faith.

> The faith to which this definition refers is not assent to a series of propositions. It may be possible to spell out some of the content of our faith in words or even to summarize it in the form of a creed. But faith as an activity is much more basic and inward than any verbal expression of it. It is a form of recognition, a way of looking at the world, an interpretative framework. To have faith is to see this world, our lives and passing events as occasions for God's demands and our response.

Strangely, Habgood succeeds more in arousing faith than in deepening and strengthening it in his preaching. If this seems odd, consider his definition of arousing faith. 'It is to open people's eyes. It is to help them to see and feel the truth of God as it is to be found in everyday happenings. It is to provide patterns of interpretation so that what may formerly have seemed meaningless or remote or irrelevant takes on a new significance. The preacher is thus acting as an interpreter, showing his congregation the world as he sees it in the light of Christ. His primary appeal is to the imagination; the truth which concerns him is the truth which lives.'

If Habgood does not concern himself with the results of his preaching, he is treading on firm theological soil. The spiritual result of preaching lies beyond the preacher's vision and control. It is good that it is so. The preacher appears to count for little in the record of the greater conversions of Christian history. The sermons of St Ambrose impressed, but did not convince, Augustine. No preacher brought St Francis to Christ; or Martin Luther, or Ignatius Loyola – or John Bunyan and John Wesley. These men are not trophies of someone's spiritual warfare. So Habgood perseveres, doing his best to illuminate the world around him, pointing away from man to God and giving Christ the opportunity to do what he will with both the preacher's words and those who listen. It is all part of the 'mystery of preaching'. And preaching it always is! There are no little chats from Habgood. When he hears of sermonettes and chats instead of sermons he is inclined to reply, 'Blessed is the man who aims at nothing, for he shall not be disappointed.'

After the teacher and the preacher there is the pastor. One of the functions of the pastor is to be a moral adviser. This role is filled with possibilities and dangers. People's expectations of priestly wisdom are often grossly inflated, despite much evidence and case histories to the contrary. The priest is supposed to have inspired but straightforward answers to 'my' problems, like some ecclesiastical agony columnist. In an age of the trained specialist can a priest have anything distinctive to say, any particular advice to offer to the troubled and the puzzled, the depressed and the anguished? Habgood thinks it important that a priest should be sensitive in his role as adviser. He must be sure that he is answering the real question, the one behind the form of words. For example, a question about the morals of contraception may be primarily aesthetic, or it may be a search for support against a partner who does not want children; or something else . . .

It may seem hackneyed to say that the priest should help or force people to make decisions for themselves, but it is true. Unfortunately, oracular pronouncements and the smack of firm principle is what is often both expected and provided.

Most personal problems are too complicated to be dealt with in this way and those who look for a simple answer are generally looking for support. Jesus did not deal with problems in this way. His thoughtful followers do not do so either. Much criticism of Habgood arises from this point. If I want buttressed support for my emotional prejudice he will not give it. If I want a plain answer, 'Yes' or 'No', to my ethical problem he will not give it. If I want a shoulder to cry on he removes it.

Why go to him? Is he no more than a listening device? Does his apparent detachment mean indifference or non-involvement? To the last question the answer is 'No'. He has said, 'Detachment means not getting confused and dominated by one's own self-interest'. A man went to see Habgood with a messy problem to which a solution was required. He expected to emerge from 'the presence' with a neat solution. Instead he was presented with a range of options and a few signposts. The visit seemed a waste of time. Some time afterwards he realized that Habgood had helped him enormously, by holding him back from rushing forward. There was only one way for him to travel and Habgood had cleared his mind, cleaned his lenses so that the perspective was unclouded before him. There was the way and he walked in it. And it was done with a peculiar mixture of deep seriousness, gentle humour and a touch that was at once light and firm.

Habgood is usually acute in distinguishing between symptoms and causes. He is also strong in his belief that people not only have problems but resources as well; and that clergy help people best by helping them use their resources in relation to their problem; that they should never do for others what they can do for themselves; that people change slowly, and with difficulty; that resistance and resentment need not be signs of failure, but signs that real learning is taking place.

Some clergy appear to accumulate 'case loads' like professional social workers. Their spiritual surgeries are crowded and the unceasing feverish activity in which they are engaged appears to have as much to do with fulfilling some emotional need of their own as with helping the person who has come, burdened with care and woe, for counsel. These spiritual surgeries are not the confessional where penitents go for a scouring of the soul and leave with absolution; neither are they places where there is real spiritual confrontation and penetration between two people.

Habgood tries to discourage the clergy from 'welfare tampering', advising that such matters be left to the professionals. But many of these professionals are Christians. And they, who are exercising a professional pastoral care to their fellows, should themselves find a care, from and by the clergy, which takes their spiritual and intellectual needs into account and speaks the language they are accustomed to use. They in their turn will be able to help the many wounded Christians who find a home in the Church, but who are too psychologically and spiritually injured to carry much witness to the world, and who can occupy a disproportionate amount of the clergy's time.

All this releases the clergy for doing what no social or other professional worker can do. In the moral and social climate of the 1960s and beyond, the priest's role as moral adviser is both highlighted and obscured. The falsely called 'New Morality' was the country of the radical. Looking at it from the other shore the purveyors of the New Morality were accused of smiling tolerantly at adultery, finding excuses for murder and calling sins 'imperfections' or 'failings'. 'Miserable sinners' became interesting cases.

The rigorists appeared to be in an historical cul-de-sac holding fast to a morality that no longer explained and answered the tortuous problems of the age. Habgood reads carefully. He was as wary of the jargon-dispensing advocates of the New Morality as he was of the cliché-ridden shibboleths of the rigorist line. He had no doubt that the priest was there as reconciler and started from the stark statement with which he began an article on 'Forgiveness' (*Theology*, September 1968): 'Christianity is about the forgiveness of sins.' He is concerned about the nature of forgiveness:

> Superficially, the command to forgive seems quite straightforward. Yet forgiveness can be, and often has been, presented in ways which make it seem intolerable. So long as a man thinks of himself as capable of forgiving, he sets

himself up as superior to those who need to be forgiven. He graciously offers a gift of tolerance in such a way as to humiliate those to whom it is extended. And tolerance under these conditions is received as an unconscious expression of arrogance . . . True Christian forgiveness is only possible on the basis that we ourselves are equally involved in the evil we seek to forgive – and are forgiven! This is totally different from forbearance or tolerance or condescension. It is the admission that the impossible can happen, that new life and hope can grow out of the entail of evil in which all of us are caught. Puzzlement about individual and corporate responsibility is a necessary prelude to *this* kind of forgiveness; and so is the recognition of pluralism, the placing in religious perspective of the multitude of rules and conventions which seem so important at the time we are confronted by them. True forgiveness lies beyond morality; like sin, it is a religious rather than a moral concept.

Once again Habgood appears to slip off the hook of directness or to take us to the kernel of the problem, depending on one's view. It has been said that Christian morals are not an attempt to practise a virtue which we all naturally admire, but an attempt to live a life which is supernaturally enabled. Habgood would not quarrel with that.

Reconciling people to themselves and to God is a primary aim of Habgood's ministry through teaching, preaching and advising. This is not done by remaining well inside the ecclesiastical structures. He has always held that priests need to look for, and recognize, and respond to God's activity in the world, independent as it may be of church auspices.

Habgood has never been jealous of God's activity outside the Church. Indeed, he is often at greatest ease and most effective when he is working with small groups of people completely independent of the ecclesiastical embrace. Nowhere is this more apparent than in considering some of the complex ethical issues of our time.

7

The Mingling of Minds

During the 1960s the Church of England, through its Board for Social Responsibility, was instrumental in producing some of the most imaginative and penetrating reports of the period on moral issues. Each was a major contribution to the subject under scrutiny and some led to changes in the law of the land. The reports came thick and fast and included *Ought Suicide to be a Crime?* (1959); *Artificial Insemination by Donor* (1960); *Sterilization: An Ethical Enquiry* (1962); *Punishment* (1963); *Decisions about Life and Death* (1965); *Abortion: An Ethical Discussion* (1965); *Fatherless by Law? The Law and the Welfare of Children designated Illegitimate* (1966). There was also the report of a group, appointed by the Archbishop of Canterbury, entitled *Putting Asunder: A Divorce Law for Contemporary Society* (1966).

There are some people who pollinated many or most of the groups including Robert Mortimer (Bishop of Exeter), Miss Josephine Barnes, R. M. Hare (Professor of Moral Philosophy in the University of Oxford), Basil Mitchell (then Fellow and Tutor of Keble College, Oxford), G. B. Bentley (Canon of Windsor) and G. R. Dunstan. Above all there was Ian Thomas Ramsey, then Nolloth Professor at Oxford but later Bishop of Durham (1966 to 1972). His name can also be found in the major study on *The Family in Contemporary Society* (1958) for the Lambeth Conference, the force and excellence of which changed the perspective of the Church.

It is the sort of company in which one might expect to see Habgood's name. The fact that one will look in vain is simply because one is looking in the wrong place and misunderstanding his particular gifts. Ending his inaugural lecture to the British Medical Association Conference in Cyprus in April

1972, Ian Ramsey said, with reference to the moral problems facing the medical profession:

> Moral decisions in the complex and novel situations with which contemporary medicine abounds need what I have called . . . transdisciplinary groups of various kinds. With each and every moral-medical problem of sufficient complexity we shall need all the relevant disciplines and professions brought to bear on it, in order that there can be a deeper grappling with the empirical facts, and a further elucidating of moral principles, so that in due course, by the marriage of both, we can expect from such a group creative moral decisions of a novel kind.
>
> Do let us realize that these consultative groups are not committees: they are not committees where decisions are reached by majority views. Consultative groups are more like research groups from which we hope to gain some creative advance. Nor do such groups compromise the physician's or the surgeon's responsibility. The decision in the end must be taken by the person who is to carry out the action, be he physician or surgeon. But a consultative group enables that decision to be the better informed, and therefore the more responsible.

Ramsey asserted with conviction that medical-moral problems were 'a special case of the struggle and turmoil which is the price we are all paying for a new civilization. It might be said that it is not so much new problems with which we are confronted as old problems in greater number and greater complexity, whose outlines are the same but whose details are different and vastly more complicated.'

Shortly before his death Ian Ramsey was advocating the formation of local groups of medical and other experts to study and give advice on current medical/ethical problems. It is not in the committee where one should look for Habgood (although in committee he is a better chairman than a member), but in the inter-disciplinary group. Succeeding Ramsey as Bishop of Durham, he was soon to be found leading a group set up in March 1973 under the auspices of the Newcastle Regional Hospital Board. Over the years the group grew and broadened but a nucleus of disciplines and insights was always there – usually a consultant obstetrician and gynaecologist, a consultant paediatrician, a consultant physician, a hospital services administrator, a regional nurse, a member of the university, the regional statistician, a lay member and a Roman Catholic priest. Habgood was always chairman. Other experts, for example a medical physicist or consultant ophthalmologist, were co-opted for particular studies.

Habgood was not only chairman but usually the scribe too. This ensured that any findings of the group stimulated a wider audience. He is at home and at ease in these interdisciplinary groups. The subjects under review are clearly defined at the outset and the objectives are realistically limited. Mental agility, technical expertise and moral sensitivity pervade the atmosphere. Woolly thinking and grapeshot are absent. Each member is expected to study the problem by reading specified reports and books and by making a complete contribution to the discussions at meetings. They represent no one but themselves, but by the high professional qualifications and positions which they hold they are likely to make a contribution that will be respected even when questioned. Consensus is not the aim. Agreement materializes more naturally. Habgood contributes to the discussions as well as chairing the group. It is not the usual kind of chairmanship, moving a meeting along to a desired or required conclusion. It is the kind which keeps the two dimensions of the group – medicine and ethics – in focus.

In one report, 'Ethics of selective treatment of spina bifida' (published in *The Lancet*, 11 January, 1975), the group had picked up one of the provocative but untested conclusions of a pamphlet on *Care of the Child with Spina Bifida* (1973), published by the Department of Health and Social Security, which stated: 'A decision not to operate implies the existence of a co-ordinated medical and nursing policy which recognized the emotional and ethical problems involved.' Treatment of this subject went straight to the nub of medical practice.

The traditional aims of medicine – the prevention of suffering and the preservation of life – are suddenly blurred. In an extended and wider-embracing version of the subject published as 'Prolongation of life in the deformed newborn' (forming the main part of *The Journal of the North East England Faculty* of the Royal College of General Practitioners, September 1975) the scene was set:

> Until the last two decades few ethical problems existed in relation to these newborn babies. The majority of those with severe abnormalities or who have suffered damage during delivery died during the newborn period or in early childhood. Advances in medical treatment, antibiotics, and the developments of anaesthetic and surgical techniques applicable to the newly born have changed this situation. Many children who would previously have died survive as a result of treatment to a life of dependence, deformity and disability. It is for this reason that an ethical dilemma arises. Should deformed newborn babies who can never be restored to normality be actively treated or should treatment be withheld in the knowledge that although the majority will die a few may survive with increased disability?
>
> The general ethical problem may be broken down into several practical issues. The first is simply whether doctors have a moral obligation to give all available treatment to such babies, or whether active treatment should be reserved for selected patients? If selection is acceptable, what factors in any individual should be considered when a decision about treatment is made? Detailed medical data relating findings during the newborn period to a long-term disability are now available for some conditions and these do allow rational selection on clinical grounds. But should social factors be considered as well? Increasing information is becoming available about the social and emotional impact of conditions such as myelomeningocele upon the child and the family. For example, physical problems associated with the day-to-day management of the child often are magnified by poor housing and financial hardship; frequent hospital admissions and outpatient visits disrupt family routine and deprive other children of parental supervision; marital relationships become strained, sexual difficulties develop and parental health deteriorates.

There are other problems too. Who is or should be involved in making 'the' decision? How can parents co-operate in decision-making immediately after a deformed birth, when they are in shock, grief and confusion? And what about the child for whom no active treatment is indicated? If life should be terminated, how should it be done?

The group asked what might be the long-term consequences of creating a medical environment in which judgements concerning pain and happiness were the sole criteria for making decisions about life and death.

> Are doctors willing or able to take upon themselves the onus of deciding what condition or quality of life is acceptable for their patients? The present balance between the aims of medicine, though it creates conflicts and may be impossible to maintain under extreme circumstances, nevertheless acts as a safeguard against the subtle acquisition of power over life and death which hitherto the medical profession have neither wanted nor been granted.

While the group considered the different arguments for the happiness of a family with a deformed baby, for the baby itself and the wider society, another approach to ethics impinged on the group's thinking.

> The assertion of overriding moral principles – for example, the principle of the sanctity of human life or, more generally, the principle of respect for human personality – can seem to introduce an arbitrary authoritarian note into the discussion which should be open and uncommitted. Yet in fact such principles simply reflect what most people believe to be true of human beings – namely, that they *are* valuable and therefore their lives *ought* to be respected. Behind such statements lie centuries of Christian teaching about the nature of man. The classic expression of the value of human personality is contained in the Christian assertion that Christ died for everybody, no matter who they are, and that therefore in the eyes of God everybody counts. Even for those who cannot assent to their religious basis, such claims have importance. Furthermore, this approach to ethics has its supreme virtue just at the point where the

> other approach is weakest – namely, in the attitude it encourages towards minorities.

At the point of greatest sensitivity the questions of suffering and the uniqueness of the individual surface and merge. Habgood does not dodge them but neither does he give unambiguous answers to the questions. It remains a troubled area for him and for anyone concerned with medical ethics. Giving a Christian view of medical ethics in a paper to a medical ethics education conference of the General Medical Council (published in the *Journal of Medical Ethics*, March 1985), Habgood has this to say about suffering: 'This is a subject on which Christians need to be cautious, because there have been times when Christianity has seemed to encourage an unhealthy resignation to suffering, and there is a sad history of Christian opposition to many pain-relieving techniques. But when all this has been admitted, there remain some profound ethical issues about the extent to which *some* suffering has to be accepted as an inevitable part of any mature life, and so used as a basis for spiritual growth.' He is rightly concerned with society's obsession with the evasion of suffering and asks: 'How far is it right, for example, to tranquillize away the experience of grief?'

In the same paper Habgood deals with theological insights which should be at the disposal of doctors to help them make decisions. He is also concerned with the style in which decisions are made.

> Doctors, so I believe, are more concerned about ethics than those in many other professions, because they have harder decisions to make, and ones which bear more directly on the lives of individuals with whom they are personally involved. And this can be a crushing burden. Hence the need to share it. Hence also the need for some inner resources to cope with the dilemmas and to bear the pain of having to choose between evils, and having to forgo doing all that they know might have been done had time, skill, resources and circumstances been different.
>
> The real resources of theology lie not in some intellectual scheme, but in the awareness of a power greater than our power, a care for individuals greater than our own care,

and a forgiveness greater than our own capacity for failure and error, which makes it possible for us to live with ourselves without complacency and without despair.

It is through the findings of groups such as the Newcastle one that doctors, nurses and members of hospital management committees find both support and direction. In the case of spina bifida the group concluded that the doctor has no ethical obligation to treat cases in which the likely benefits are very dubious. 'Thus in the present state of medical knowledge the policy of selection for the treatment of spina bifida is in our opinion justified . . . No general statements of this kind can override the responsibility of the doctors concerned to make particular decisions in individual cases.'

Another issue considered by the Newcastle group was sterilization of the mentally-handicapped. This subject is a growing rather than a diminishing one. The days of the asylum are, thankfully, gone. At that time the mentally handicapped were removed from society, segregated by sex and 'locked' away. Now there is a new philosophy of care for the mentally handicapped which allows considerable freedom to form relationships and in the mixing of sexes. Unfortunately, the available guidance on how to use that freedom has been scanty. The Newcastle report (largely written by Habgood) put it succinctly: 'The more the mentally handicapped are encouraged to enjoy a normal social life, the more they are likely to want to form either permanent or casual unions and the more serious the ethical implications of depriving them of their natural fulfilment.'

Many moderately or mildly handicapped people are sexually active. Those who care for and about them tend to be concerned about hereditary defects in any offspring a couple might have, where one or both of the partners is mentally handicapped. But that concern should not lead to a genetic argument for sterilization. The offspring may be nearer the norm in intelligence than their parents. The 'genetic argument' is one which can lead to 'genetic control' and twentieth-century history shows the devilish outcome when control is turned into national policy.

Then there is the question of parental inadequacy, but this

is not limited to subnormal parents. The Children's Act of 1975 makes it clear that a mother does not have the right to bring up her child if she is unable to provide him or her with a healthy and stimulating environment. In society generally the number of 'inadequate' parents is rising rapidly. Among the mentally handicapped there are special difficulties. The working group put it thus:

> Contraception may fail, not only through incompetence in managing it, but through inability to see the connection between the desired birth of children and the long-term problems of their upbringing. The case for sterilizing those whose inadequacy has been clearly demonstrated is stronger than the case for sterilizing those who have borne no children at all. It can also be argued that consent for sterilization may be more readily understood by those who have already experienced parenthood.

Men pose a different dilemma. The man may be persuaded to be sterilized when two mentally handicapped people are married or have a long-standing relationship. But what of the mild or moderately handicapped but promiscuous male either in an institution or in the community? He may be a menace, a threat and a danger. What does one do? Control the situation by drugs, sterilize or surgically castrate a promiscuous male? Anything that is irreversible, and by the nature of the operation results in changed personality, is to be avoided. It is not surprising that the working group advocated control by appropriate drugs.

As for mentally subnormal females, the group considered that only proven parental incapacity, coupled with an inability to manage contraceptives reliably, would seem to provide justification for sterilization. 'This conclusion carries with it the corollary that adequate support must be provided by the community for mentally handicapped parents with children.'

Common to this and other reports from the group was the statement that decisions should only be made as a result of a formal consultation procedure in which the patient's long-term interests are represented. Too little heed is given to the involved processes of consultation which take place over particular cases. Care and responsibility are natural partners in the majority of hospitals. The occasional scandal which captures the headlines must not be allowed to blur that fact. Nevertheless, with an increasing number of individuals involved in a single case there is a greater chance of patients' histories and records becoming too public. We have moved a long way from the one-to-one professional relationship between doctor and patient. But have we moved too far?

Habgood and the Newcastle group considered the subject of confidentiality and published their findings in *The Lancet* (13 August 1983). They recognized that with the coming of the National Health Service medicine had been bureaucratized. Strangely, the group seemed insufficiently sensitive to the importance of confidentiality from the patient's point of view. Apart from the priest in the confessional, the doctor's or consultant's surgery and the psychiatrist's 'couch' have been thought of as bastions of complete trust. There one pours out one's heart, describes one's symptoms and reveals all in more ways than the obvious one – but often one does that too! The relationship which used to exist between the individual general practitioner and the patient has largely gone. The GP is simply in a medical chain. The report of the group states: 'Mistrust and disappointment are bound to result in patients who retain a traditional image of health care which no longer matches reality.' But the image was the reality. It is glib to say 'it would be reassuring to such patients to have the system explained and be told something about the limits of the medical team'. It is the explanation which makes them uneasy and mistrustful.

Yet there are great benefits for both doctor and patient in opening up a case for wider scrutiny. Symptoms take on a different perspective when considered by different professional groups. But these different groups have different aims, share different assumptions and are likely to put their information to different uses. As the report states,

> A case conference that included teachers and police as well as doctors and social workers would have to consider the patient's different expectations of each profession and might well share different confidences. The professionals might

> feel they were being misled by one another if information were deliberately withheld, and it could be argued that it is in the interests of patients that they be dealt with as whole persons, rather than having separate aspects of their problems dealt with by unrelated groups. On the other hand, it can be argued that total care smacks of paternalism; that it is precisely by dealing with different professions in different ways that individuals are able to retain some privacy and assert their autonomy.

As bureaucracy has increased, the amount of information about a patient has increased with it. Computerization of medical records is a spectre looming large. Strict confidentiality is no longer a fact, perhaps not possible, and, some argue, perhaps not desirable. The greyest of areas surrounds the patient's records. Legally, the file belongs to the Secretary of State, with the District Authority as its custodian. The information contained in the file does not belong to anyone. The doctors compile the information as NHS employees and so have no legal rights over it. Contrary to what some people think, the patient owns neither the file nor the information.

The conclusions reached by Habgood and the group on the limited task they had set themselves were:

> It is important not to mislead patients about the degree of confidentiality which it is reasonable to expect in an organization as large and complex as the NHS. Information given in strict confidence, however, must be honoured. The importance of confidentiality should be emphasized in the training of all NHS employees, who should also undertake to observe confidentiality as part of their contract of employment, with penalties built in if this undertaking is not entirely honoured. Legal control of access to information can set limits on the exchange of information as well as facilitating it. Present assumptions within the NHS were formed in a period when relationships both inside and outside the profession were much simpler. In the light of reactions to the proposed Police and Criminal Evidence Bill (1982), we suggest that thought be given to the question of the ownership of information, as opposed to the ownership of documents or tapes on which it may be recorded.

> Patients also have their own legal interests in medical information about themselves.

Once again the purpose of the multi-disciplinary group was to make a small but significant contribution to a growing debate. Not for them the trumpetry of blueprints and wide-ranging proposals which would recede as quickly as one day's news is replaced by the next. The Habgood model, and that of any working group with which he was associated, was to set limited achievable objectives. The findings of groups and working parties appeared in journals and periodicals read by the medical profession. The aim was to stimulate thought and discussion and always to present the ethical choices on medical subjects. They kept their arguments strong and cogent and their conclusions realistic. There was never any doubt that they were concerned with medical *ethics*.

Mention has been made earlier that Habgood wrote many of the reports himself and sometimes when published they carry his name as author. He writes with clarity, even pungently, on topics where there is a technical content. One such study, 'The ethics of resource allocation: a case study' (published in the *Journal of Medical Ethics*, March 1983) analysed the factors involved in a series of decisions by the Newcastle Area Health Authority concerning the future of Walkergate Hospital. Habgood described the general background to the study, a background which remains all too relevant.

> It is often stated that the problems of the National Health Service could be resolved by the allocation of additional monies. Indeed, in the past, this has frequently been the case, at least superficially. The reality now is that the rising costs of health care are of concern to governments throughout the Western world, and produce similar problems no matter how the system is funded or how much is already spent. In a declining economy the problems are especially acute, and are compounded by the rigidity often imposed on systems when they are under financial constraint.
>
> There is no simple way of deciding, when the demand exceeds the supply, how available resources ought to be allocated. In the past, allocations appear to have been

> made on the basis of tradition, evolution, emotion and optimism.
>
> The traditional basis of medicine is that of saving life. The so-called 'acute' specialities have therefore been awarded priority. Many of the problems with which they currently cope, however, are less than acute and many lives are incapable of being saved.

This particular case study looked at Walkergate Hospital in Newcastle which faced closure and redevelopment as a result of a projected shortfall in income by the local area health authority. A confidential report found its way into the restive hands of the press before the process of public consultation had been started. The media ensured that the issue became a controversy, and stances were quickly adopted so that different positions became warring factions. What followed illustrated the complex balance of factors, political, professional, administrative, psychological, as well as public opinion, which impinges on a decision of this nature.

A major feature was whether the then general hospital specializing in dermatology, geriatrics, ear, nose and throat, ophthalmology and dental patients should be rebuilt as a geriatic centre. The acute services would be redistributed among other Newcastle hospitals. The working party found there was no easy way to resolve the various conflicts of interest, notably in this particular case the conflicting demands of acute and chronic medicine. Difficult decisions were made more difficult by the over-rigid division of medicine into compartments, by mistrust between the medical profession and administrators, and by the inordinately long time-scale of the decision-making process. The group admitted: 'The moral of the story is a confused one. An individual doctor asked to decide between using limited resources for heart surgery or providing facilities for old people might find such a choice intolerable. Committees find it equally hard to make clear choices about priorities, and to stick to them, though they have the advantage of being further from the distressing personal and individual factors which weigh more heavily on those facing actual choices about particular patients. Concentration on more immediate but less personal items, such as adjustments, costs and bargaining powers, enables decisions to be made, though in retrospect the process often looks messy and the eventual decisions less than ideal.

'When the inherent difficulty of the process is compounded by lack of trust, in-fighting and uncertainties of popular feeling, it is not surprising that a practical solution which avoids the main underlying issues is grasped with relief.'

The group brought some of the underlying issues to the surface and examined some basic principles involved in this study. Perhaps even more important, they articulated something about the needs of people to have symbols of the pricelessness of human life. In most of the findings of the Newcastle group's reports reference is made to this. Here, for example,

> Huge resources may be used in a single rescue operation, which if distributed more rationally might in the long run save more lives, though in less dramatic ways. It is as if popular feeling needs from time to time some visible symbolic reminder that no price is too high in matters of life and death, while at the same time it is recognized implicitly that most people's day-to-day actions belie this valuation.
>
> Perhaps medicine, too, needs its dramatic, and expensive, symbols of 'total care'. Apart from their research value, occasional examples of 'heroic medicine' underline the imperative to spare no effort in saving life. No doubt each doctor will continue to think of his own patients as suitable recipients of such care. But administrators, with a more distant view, ought to be able to distinguish between what it is possible to maintain as a norm, and what belongs to the category of the exceptional. The resulting compromise may seem unfair. It is an unfairness which is commonly accepted in other areas of life, however, and there is no inherent reason why the public should not be educated to accept that the most advanced and expensive forms of medicine cannot be available to all. The fact that they are available to some expresses an intention and a hope, and may pave the way for others to share in them. But the norm has to be set at a lower level.

This is another example of Habgood's cautious realism and steady vision. A problem is confronted and dissected with a surgeon's knife. It is examined with care and then stitched back up again. There is no instant treatment leading to certain cure. The problem remains, but the possibilities of solving it are heightened in proportion to lowered expectations. The ethical dimension is introduced as both ideal and lamp-post (to illuminate, not to lean on). Many members of the different branches of the medical profession have been encouraged by these reports. They looked at issues from a new angle. There were other reports, for example 'Ethical problems of repetitive research' (published in the *Journal of Medical Ethics*, 1977, no. 3), which sounded a cautionary note against repeatedly using the same patients for clinical research. When patients are used as medical guinea pigs, are they always aware of the exact nature of the research? Ethical committees should be more stringent in their form of inquiry and in their giving of consent.

Another report, *The Principles which should guide the Ethical Committees of the Area Health Authorities*, disclosed a lamentable lack of statistical information locally which, if repeated on a national scale, would mean duplicated research, little sharing of findings and a resulting waste of time, energy and financial resources. There should be a national study to assess the balance and distribution of medical research; to assess its value; to assess the relationship between the benefit to the patient and the cost to the patient (in terms of danger, discomfort and inconvenience); and to provide guidance to ethical committees. Standard forms for application for approach on ethical grounds to undertake clinical research investigations were suggested, and details of information were set out in draft form. A shortened version of the report appeared in *The Lancet* (14 January 1978).

Another delicate issue was considered, namely, the relationship between the medical profession and the media, which began to look at the possibility of drawing up guidelines for the approach by the media to the medical profession, and vice versa, in the hope that these might develop into a mutually acceptable code of conduct.

The issues are not ones which propelled Habgood into

prominence. They are not ones on which a bishop or an archbishop is asked to 'pronounce'. In the public mind ethical issues are not moral issues. The latter supposedly comprises such issues as abortion, euthanasia, divorce and artificial insemination, which will be considered in the next chapter.

Here, for the moment, we see Habgood in a setting in which he has much to give and enjoys giving it. Even so, amidst technical and medical problems he never loses sight of the theological contribution he must make to any subject under scrutiny. That is his distinctive contribution and it is always in the indicative rather than in the imperative mood. That is not all, for as he wrote in one of the contributions to the *Dictionary of Medical Ethics* (1977):

> The final words in a Christian account of ethics must be forgiveness and grace. This is not only because any workable ethic must make provision for failure, but mainly because part of the human predicament is the fact that many decisions entail choices between evils, and even the best actions leave many claims unmet. Finite human beings have to do the best they can. To live within the context of forgiveness and grace makes it possible to accept the inevitable ambiguities of human conduct, without lapsing into complacency or cynicism, or losing hold of the vision of some greater good.

8

Passionate Moderate

In her essay on 'The sovereignty of good' Iris Murdoch says: 'The love which brings the right answer is an exercise of justice and realism and really *looking*' – and, one might add, really *listening*.

The need for church leaders both to look and to listen before reaching for their pens or opening their mouths is as necessary as it is difficult and nowhere more so than on moral questions.

When Habgood accepted the call to 'public office' he knew what he was doing. Preaching at the Judges' Service in Durham Cathedral (10 October 1982) he said:

> Public office makes us seem larger than life. Most people shrink from public responsibility. It is always much easier just to think of oneself and to fight one's own battles and pursue one's own interests. But those of us who choose, or are chosen, to serve our fellow-citizens in public office have ceased just to be individuals. We carry the hopes and fears and difficulties and aspirations and frustrations and disagreeablenesses of many others. They project onto us all sorts of fantasies about the kind of people we are, and what we can do, and the motives from which we act, and the degree to which we succeed or fail.

How does Habgood cope with the incessant demand made upon him that every problem should have a solution, and every question a simple, quotable answer? Not by parrying and not by pronouncing! Looking and listening is his style, and writing or speaking when he has made up his mind and if he feels he has anything to say. These are not easy times for liberal-thinking people. Habgood is well aware of the easy slander of 'woolly-minded, trendy do-gooders' which heads in the direction of liberals.

In one of his 'Bishop's Letters' to the Diocese of Durham (May 1974) he refers to the liberal dilemma. The subject was abortion but the argument applies generally.

> The man in the middle, the liberal-minded Christian, who wishes to be compassionate towards those who suffer or are in danger through unwanted pregnancies, but who at the same time sees that there are important principles at stake, finds himself pushed hither and thither, easily conned by those with axes to grind, frequently agreeing to compromises which are then abused.
>
> The history of liberalizing legislation is full of such examples. The laws on gambling, the 1969 Divorce Reform Act, the relaxation of censorship in the arts, the latest Government decision to issue free contraceptives, can all be defended on good and reasonable grounds. Cumulatively they are making deep changes in the character of our society, some good and some bad. For their moral justification they depend on the drawing of fine distinctions, which are then for the most part ignored in practice. The end result may be to create a society which is superficially more free, but which in fact puts enormous pressure on individuals to conform to a new style whether they like it or not.

Habgood asks, 'What is the liberal to do?' and says, 'I believe it is important not to be cynical about our present-day society, and not to react in fright away from the consequences of our attempts to make it more humane. Our Christian gospel is about freedom, freedom bought at an appalling cost but not, despite its dangers, to be exchanged for something safer and more comfortable. This is what the Epistle to the Galatians is about. Those who have learnt to live by grace dare not revert to the safety and simplicity of a rigid legalism.'

Habgood holds that moral conflict may be a sign of health. 'Conflict may be valuable in making us all eternally vigilant about the freedoms which matter to us.' For him the real danger is 'moral sloth, the passive acceptance of the way in which society is going, the flashy permissiveness which is not the fruit of genuine caring but of "couldn't care less".'

By this kind of liberalism we are taken a long way from its popular image which suggests that permissiveness is in effect an unthinking and unprincipled radicalism. But we are brought to the core of Habgood's strength or, as his opponents would have it, his weakness. At the core, words such as 'compromise', 'freedom' and 'reconciliation' are found. The words have always been there and with increased responsibility they have assumed greater importance and are under greater attack. Herein rests the difficulty, as Habgood was quick to discover when becoming a bishop. Words such as 'compromise' and 'freedom' are not much help if they are used by different people acting on different assumptions and living by different rules. Moreover, the current times encourage slogan throwers and jargon dispensers, people who splatter verbal bombast or who coin snappy phrases.

Once when discussing words and concepts such as justice and freedom, Habgood observed that such words became missiles and were used to give momentum without any serious examination of what is being said. The mass media feed on oversimplification and the news and views purveyed in and by the media have an increasingly pre-digested flavour to them. This worries Habgood, for he sees it in the Church as well as in society and politics. As we stumble towards the end of the century, exaggeration takes the place of accuracy. Reflection and thought are nudged aside. The manipulator and decision-maker has no time for such luxuries. In his 'Bishop's Letter' for April 1977 Habgood faced this problem. While admitting that exaggeration may be an occasional useful tool for teaching, he goes on: 'As a way of life it not only distorts the truth but threatens human relationships. If everything is painted in the same violent colours, nothing can be seen for what it is, and nobody outside the inner circle of enthusaists can be accepted for what they are.

'Perhaps it is a sign of middle age to want to be a passionate moderate. A moderate believes that anyone can make mistakes – including himself. He therefore tries to hear all sides and keep the balance. He avoids exaggeration.

> Unkind critics have sometimes described this attitude as like 'sitting on the fence with both ears to the ground'. A fairer description compares it to riding a bicycle, which at least makes it clear that it is not a recipe for sitting still and doing nothing. Passionate moderation entails a passion to be fair, fair above all to the truth. It is a form of self-control mingled with honesty and humility. It is not one of those exciting virtues which enables people to bang about and feel important. In fact it is a rather quiet virtue which may lead those who do not possess it to react with impatience. But I suggest our world needs it rather badly.

Habgood is describing himself.

Habgood is concerned with the choices which politicians have to make, choices that affect the lives of everyone. Politicians of the 'middle way' have his particular sympathy and attention. The strident tone and posturing attitudes of some other politicians disturb him to the point of fear. How can the church leader help the politician? For Habgood, first, by listening. There are many opportunities open to a bishop. I select just one example.

Western democracy has been under strain for some time. The vast majority of the world's nations have rejected it. Habgood was one of a select group of about thirty politicians, high-ranking civil servants, and political commentators from both sides of the Atlantic, attending a 1976 conference under the auspices of the Ditchley Foundation. The chairman was Edward Heath. The theme was 'Values and decision-making in modern democratic societies'. This stimulating gathering hit Habgood in an unexpected and unintentional way. He realized how slender was his equipment to enter into political discussions at the level of the conference and admits: 'This was not only a personal failing, though it included that element. Current Christian thinking on social and political matters does not relate easily to the concerns of practical politicians, and there was little respect for what were believed to be official Christian attitudes, even among those who are themselves Christians. The Churches were felt to be in constant danger of moralizing or looking for simplistic solutions.'

The politicians were under strain too. Does Parliament any longer represent the true centre of power? Who constitute the new power groups and how can they be drawn into the decision-making machinery? How can any government fulfil the unreal expectations of the electorate during times of actual recession or limited growth? Habgood was surprised at the unanimity which greeted the policy of continued economic growth. Wealth can be distributed and social improvements made only though a policy of overall growth because that is where the new money comes from to do new things. Habgood is not convinced. He says:

> We have to rid ourselves of the idea of limitless possibilities. There needs to be more public debate on the true cost of various policies, and in particular the public need to be made more aware of the extent to which politics is the art of compromise. But how do we distinguish between reasonable compromise and unprincipled opportunism? How can we be flexible, and yet retain a core of conviction? The Churches, with their tendencies to absolutism, have not helped as much as they might in working out a morality of compromise.

Habgood constantly returns to the theme of compromise. In an important article, 'Theological reflections on compromise' (published in *Explorations in Ethics and International Relations: Essays in Honour of Sydney D. Bailey*, edited by Nicholas A. Sims, 1981), he defends the concept of compromise while recognizing its limitations and dangers. The mean between statesmanlike compromise and unprincipled surrender is never easy to calculate. Habgood theologically justifies compromise to the point of its being seen as an expression of faith. In almost everything he writes on the subject he reveals a great deal of his own mental processes and a little of himself. Thus, 'the more the Church regards itself as possessing the objective treasures of grace, the less it need be damaged by the absence of personal holiness among its members, and the compromises into which it is forced by the pressure of events. The Church is holy, but its holiness is compatible with its role as a school for sinners, rather than a society for saints.'

Or again, we find Habgood returning to a constant theme,

that of obliqueness. It is an element in compromise. It is a way of looking at problems and a way of facing them. Superficially, it may appear that one is deflecting difficult questions. But look more closely. Why should it be seen as a sign of strength to be the man with the answers? (Usually they are platitudes and people too easily settle for them.) A Christian should look at how Jesus answered questions.

> Jesus spoke in parables. Straight answers to straight questions are rare in his teaching. His favourite method was to illuminate some problem by putting it in a fresh context, and then pass it back to the questioner. To reply to the question 'Who is my neighbour?' by telling the story of the Good Samaritan is to do more than provide a vivid illustration of some simple truth about neighbours being people in trouble. The story reverberates on many levels, can be interpreted in many ways and allows the hearer to identify himself with more than one character. There is a real sense, therefore, in which the hearer provides his own answer to the original question. An oblique shaft of light shows him where he stands and what he is. It helps to reveal God by conveying an awareness of multiple layers of meaning in which the hearer himself is involved . . . Obliqueness, far from being a disadvantage in religious discourse, may be the only way to express the inexpressible.

Habgood admits that there are times when the will of God is clear and definite, but one should not be fretting when it is not clear. A God who reveals himself in hints and glimpses is infinitely more worshipful and lovable than a God who is constantly writing new Tablets of Law.

In political and moral terms Habgood is referring to compromise as a means of resolving competing interests. Yet he clarifies that by stating:

> When the context is a conflict between evils rather than between interests, compromise contains an element of connivance with evil, which is dangerous if it is allowed to continue unchecked, and eventually unnoticed. Such compromises harden into solutions which embody the evils

> from which they were intended to provide the means of escape.
>
> The emphasis on forbearance, on not pushing ahead with decisions recklessly in order to appear decisive, is the main positive factor in compromise according to this analysis. Its main negative factor is the peril of compliance and complacency.

In practical politics the big issues of the day are multi-dimensional. Politicians in particular are caught between the time-scales. In energy policy, for example, decisions have to be made looking decades ahead at the same time as responding to the constant and immediate pressures. Far-reaching decisions are often postponed because the immediate pressures are stronger. Habgood says: 'An awareness of moral time limits within which compromises are allowable may help to define the border between cautious flexibility and weak-willed procrastination.'

More than anything else Habgood urges Christian politicians to accept the paradox of grace so that they will have 'the moral courage needed to take some decisive action, without the arrogance which then refuses to admit that it might be wrong'. The parliamentary whip system has much to answer for, as has the method of voting. Not surprisingly, he advocates proportional representation.

On the subject of energy, Habgood was a member of a study group which produced a report, *Deciding about Energy Policy: Principles and Procedures for making Energy Policy in the United Kingdom* (1979). This is another multi-disciplinary group, this time of the Council for Science and Society of which Habgood is a council member. The Council's primary task is to stimulate informed public discussion in the field of the social responsibility of the scientist. It is concerned with developments in science and technology whose social consequences lie just over the horizon, where full-scale debate has hardly started, but where intensive analysis of the present and possible or probable future 'state of the art', and of the foreseeable social consequences, can suggest a range of possible responses to those who will sooner or later have to take the necessary decision. A glance at the list of members of the 'Energy' study group is sufficient to disclose the deep seriousness of the approach to the subject. They were: John Ziman (Convener), Professor of Physics, University of Bristol; Dame Elizabeth Ackroyd, Chairman, South Eastern Electricity Consultative Council; Professor Ralf Dahrendorf, Director, London School of Economics; F. R. Farmer, Safety Adviser, UK Atomic Energy Authority; Ian Fells, Professor of Energy Conversion, University of Newcastle; Habgood, then Bishop of Durham; David Henderson, Professor of Political Economy, University College, London; Baroness Jackson of Lodsworth, President, International Institute for Environment and Development; Gerald Leach, Director, Energy Project at the International Institute; Patricia Lindop, Professor of Radiobiology, Medical College of St Bartholomew's Hospital; Paul Sieghart, Chairman of the Executive Committee of Justice, British Section of the International Commission of Jurists; and Kenneth Denbigh, Director, Council for Science and Society.

Reports of the Council avoid conclusions or recommendations. The technical detail is substantial, the critical assessment acute and the observations are penetrating. The selected topics for study have a high level of human interest. They include 'Life and death before birth' – a study of the human problems arising from the use of antenatal diagnostic technology: 'Harmless weapons' – the problem of the introduction of sophisticated weapons for the control of civil disorder in Great Britain, 'New technology' – society, employment and skill. In each case, and for Habgood in the 'Energy' group, the big issue is the ethical one: on the one hand, scientific research and advance; on the other, public scepticism and anxiety. The scientist, like everybody else, must emerge from the laboratory and engage in an open discussion of values as these apply, both to the manner of the research and to the possible uses which society may make of it.

Habgood knows only too well that discussion among those who share the same expertise can do justice to the nuances of a subject, but is unlikely to result in radical criticism. Interdisciplinary discussion of the kind the 'Energy Policy' report stimulated was true to the facts and critical of the assumptions which underlay them. Again we see Habgood on favourite ground – the ethical task lies in the middle ground where conflicts of value may be expected to occur.

Energy policy includes the nuclear element. During the summer of 1976 Habgood paid an official visit to Windscale to look at the plant where spent fuel from nuclear reactors is reprocessed. This led him to contemplate the choice facing political leaders whether to opt for a nuclear future which would secure the country's energy supplies for centuries to come, or to adopt a non-nuclear option which would lead to a drastic slowing down of the rate of growth. Each has social consequences. The question to be faced was, should Britain embark on a programme of building fast-breeder nuclear reactors? At this stage he avoided making any political comment. His reflection is a Christian one. He sees the incarnation, 'not only as an act of overflowing love, but also as an act of restraint'. Writing at Christmas 1976 he suggests that the 'festival of self-indulgence is at its Christian heart a celebration of God's restraint, his scaling-down to human limitations. Restraint is not a popular theme nowadays . . . but it is here, I believe, in self-limitation as an expression of love that our appropriate Christian witness lies. And one practical example of this witness could be by cautioning our leaders against a thrusting policy of nuclear expansion.'

It may seem strange but Habgood became more widely known and increasingly used in connection with technology and nuclear issues because of a sermon! Paul Abrecht, formerly Director of the Church and Society unit of the World Council of Churches explains:

> I had not met Bishop Habgood until 1978, but I knew about his double interest in the faith-science issue (as a scientist and as a theologian). On the strength of this we invited him to be the preacher for the World Council of Churches' Conference on 'Faith, science and the future' held at the Massachusetts Institute of Technology, Cambridge, USA in July 1979. However, his eventual influence on the Conference extended beyond that. During a conference debate about Science for Peace it was decided to issue a statement putting the Conference on record against the expanding use of science and scientists for

> weapons development. A committee representing different views was named and John Habgood was asked to chair it. He did this most successfully and with great fairness and the resulting resolution was one of the most important recommendations of the Conference to the churches.

With 405 people from fifty-six countries this was the largest gathering of scientists, technologists, theologians and others ever brought together under Christian auspices to discuss mutual problems of faith and practice.

In his sermon at the conference Habgood spoke of a God who both cares and interferes, and God's interference demands responsiveness. Is this Habgood lapsing into a simplistic message? Not so! God interferes, 'subtly, in the form of a servant, so that the bruised reed is not broken and the smoking flax is not quenched. The character of God's care is that it is incarnated, localized, rooted in the world itself. Perhaps this is where some of our human work reveals its failings.' An interesting passage in the sermon concerned the search for truth and concern for God.

> If we human beings are only in some distorted fashion godlike, if we are trapped in our own particular points of view, conditioned by who we are and where we are, then it is not enough just to equate our truth with God's – and leave things there. The way to truth, to unity of perception, is much more costly than that. The gospel is that God doesn't just stand there as some sort of ultimate truth. He enters into our human points of view and shares them, and slowly bridges the gulfs between them, if we will let him, and offers us the promise of transcending them, and meanwhile bears the pain of our distortions and divisions. We too are not to be godlike spectators searching for patterns in a universe which somehow already reflects the unity of God. We are fellow-workers invited, incredibly, to share in the costly work of creating a universe. We are to 'make sense' of it: make it in the active sense, not just in the passive sense.

The two-volume report of the conference, *Faith and Science in an Unjust World* (1980), though wordy, repays reading. Habgood wrote a small (unattributable) section on 'Behaviour control' in which he asked the question, 'Is there an inviolable core of personality which cannot, or ought not, to be touched by anything which can be done to it in the name of science?' Traditional concepts of the soul presuppose that there is. They refer to that part of a person which represents ultimate individuality, which is held in being by God, and whose significance resides in its relationship with him.

The conference was the first at which Habgood experienced the global dimension. Speaking the truth in love meant for some participants expressing themselves in vituperative impatience and anger. In some reflections on this conference published as 'Can science survive?' in *Queen's Essays* (1980), Habgood expresses a degree of shock at some of the exchanges though there is still a feeling of detachment, an unwillingness to be drawn into the centre of the fray. Is it possible to have a meeting of wills without a meeting of minds? There is unease at some of the views expressed. Is there also a condescending attitude, albeit unconscious, towards those who spoke in anger, and righteous anger at that? Does the superior smile of the Englishman represent a failure to understand at a deep level the 'running out of patience' of many countries towards the West? He may later have observed in his 'Bishop's letter' (September 1979), 'We must stop squandering the world's resources, and must learn to use them more justly and with more sensitivity to the way people actually feel', but did he feel it, really feel it? Or was he – is he – too cerebral?

The fact that a man keeps his emotions in check does not mean that he does not feel deeply or strongly. It may mean that his reserves of energy are prevented from being used up in needless ways. In 1983 when Habgood had been Bishop of Durham for ten years, the Archbishop of York (Stuart Blanch) mounted the steps of Durham Cathedral pulpit to congratulate him, 'on having survived ten years in the episcopate and what is more, survived with humour and dignity in an office which can undermine the strongest constitution and cloud the clearest mind'.

Clearness of mind is worth preserving at the cost of emotional commitment. It was the mental clarity and skill in drafting reports that led the World Council of Churches to invite Habgood to chair an international public hearing on nuclear weapons and disarmament in Amsterdam in November 1981. Witnesses of the highest calibre and with diverse views gave evidence. The task of the hearing was to receive and evaluate different points of view, a task for which Habgood is supremely well fitted. Whether he would make a good judge is more questionable, but as a chairman of a gathering such as this he is of the top class. The 391-page report, *Before It's Too Late: The Challenge of Nuclear Disarmament*, was published in 1983.

We have seen Habgood's interest in nuclear technology. He is president of the British branch of an influential but little known body (and influential because little known) called the Christian Council on Approaches to Defence and Disarmament (CCADD). As Habgood explains,

> CCADD has deliberately not sought publicity; it is a small body whose aim is to think and to explore rather than to act as a pressure group. It contains pacifists and non-pacifists, experts in military matters and non-experts like myself, people of all shades of opinion and of all churches, who are united only in our Christian commitment. It has many contacts in the Ministries of Defence and at Government level in the countries where it operates, and for those engaged in the thick of actual policy-making and negotiation, it provides a fresh atmosphere, a broader perspective in which their problems can be seen.

CCADD began life in 1961 on the gentle, prodding and determined initiative of the late Robert Stopford, Bishop of London, and Rear-Admiral Anthony Buzzard, with others such as David Edwards and Kenneth Johnstone. That great Quaker ('great' seems an odd word to use for a Quaker) Sydney Bailey became a key person and very soon CCADD was undertaking technical and ethical studies. A conference in July 1963 was attended by thirty-five people including Alun Gwynne Jones (later Lord Chalfont) who was Minister of State at the Foreign and Commonwealth Office 1964–70; and Michael Howard, Professor of War Studies at the University of London 1953–61 and from 1968 a Fellow of All Souls College, Oxford. In *Explorations in Ethics* tribute is paid to

Sydney Bailey and his distinctive contribution to CCADD. It bears repetition for the light it sheds on the way CCADD works.

> First, it is largely thanks to his relations of close personal confidence with Bishop Herman Kunst [of the Federal German Republic – who was head of the military chaplaincies of his own country when he met Bailey], to his contacts in America and his painstaking work in preparing the agenda for the annual conference that the international character of CCADD has been sustained and developed and indeed enlarged to include representatives from Eastern Europe and the Third World. Secondly, under his guidance the reconciling role of the Council has been reinforced. Himself a pacifist, the humility with which he nevertheless seeks to understand and the instinctive charity that he shows towards the position of those who cannot accept the pacifist view, has made CCADD a meeting place where the two groups can really listen to one another. Serving officers and senior government officials have felt able to take part in the Council's work not least because of Sydney Bailey's expert knowledge and his ability to present critical views in terms that attract as well as compel their attention. The third contribution is the emphasis he has given to CCADD's role of making more widely available information about defence and disarmament issues with ethical implications.

It is not difficult to see why Habgood is keen about CCADD. There is no question of CCADD wagging its finger at the Church or admonishing the Foreign Office or giving the Ministry of Defence a new defence policy. It is a non-decision-making resource body and continues to attract influential people into its web. Naturally, there are tensions as in any body that is high-powered in its membership yet tends to avoid decision-making and judgement-offering. The temptation for CCADD to go 'provocative' is one that should be resisted. At a time when the volume of published literature on defence, disarmament and deterrence multiplies weekly, much of it from over-prepared positions, the need for informed comment and criticism is greater than ever.

As Habgood sees it, CCADD provides the opportunity for people with committed but diverse views to take counsel together. The fruit of reflection and stimulation is ripened in CCADD but eaten in other places. The British Group of CCADD which has a wide range of activities between conferences has never taken a particular position itself in spite of occasional intense pressure to do so. Under Habgood's presidency it will maintain that position.

The Royal Commission on Environmental Pollution (chaired by Sir Brian Flowers) published its sixth report, *Nuclear Power and the Environment*, in 1976. Habgood's presidential address to CCADD in November 1976 dealt with fast-breeder reactors. The dangers inherent in routine operation, of pollution by radioactive waste, were technically analysed. The military risks were acknowledged. Habgood had been struck by a phrase used by Sir Brian Flowers when speaking at the National Energy Conference in June 1976: 'We believe that nobody should rely for something as basic as energy on a process that produces in quantity a by-product as dangerous as plutonium.' Habgood said: 'The significance of that remark lies in the phrase "as basic as energy".' The argument, in other words, is not about a fringe benefit, however desirable, but about the resource on which the whole of an industrial society depends, and which therefore deeply influences the character of that society. An Indian physicist has written: 'Scratch any piece of technology and you will find the values and aims of the society it was designed to serve. For technology is like genetic material – it carries with it the code of the society which conceived it. This is why the choice of technology is such a crucial decision in the developing countries today. The kind of society and the kind of environment which they will create depends to a large extent on what technology they choose for the job of development.'

By the end of the address Habgood had reached a conclusion, namely that Britain should opt out of fast-breeder development. He returned to his theme of 'holding back'. 'We have for too long identified the creativeness for which man was made, with scientific and technological advance, and now need to place greater emphasis on the kind of moral spiritual restraints within which it must be exercised.' In the end the choices made by individuals and by nations will probably depend on ill-formulated beliefs about human nature, and it is on this level that Christian insights can perhaps be of most help in clarifying the issues. Are human beings resilient enough to cope with the unprecedented problems of a nuclear age and the permanent commitment which this would entail? Alternatively, is this possibly our last opportunity to reverse the current trends? Which is more fundamental as a type of Christian response – thrusting creativeness or a humble acknowledgement of human limitations?

By 1986 we find Habgood saying that the gap between the public perception of nuclear energy and the perception from within the industry might possibly be closed a little by a more trenchant analysis of the kinds of risks involved in operating nuclear plant. He draws a distinction between operational safety (i.e. that depending on the human factors), engineered safety (depending upon compensatory devices, etc.) and inherent safety (dependent upon fundamental design). The need to move in the direction of greater inherent safety is crucial. Habgood notes:

> There are now only ten types of nuclear reactor operating in the whole world. Design in other words has become fossilized or, as I put it, has gone into an evolutionary cul-de-sac because the financial and political consequences of making fundamental design changes are too great. The only way out of the cul-de-sac it seems to me is to experiment with new generations of small reactors which would be less expensive to produce and might find a ready market in parts of the world where some nuclear energy would be useful, but where the massive plants we have at the moment would only be an embarrassment.

Habgood, and those who think with or like him, hold up visions of ultimate ends and ideal solutions. He says: 'Those who live at the sharp end of the world's affairs constantly need reminding of these visions, if they are not just to drift along under the pressure of events. But Christian insights can only help if those who offer them genuinely acknowledge the complexity of the problems to which they are applied.' Habgood endeavours to understand, and his experiences in meeting people in study groups and informal conferences continually sharpens his thinking. He is ever sensitive to those people who have to make decisions. Preaching at a Falklands Thanksgiving Service in Durham Cathedral (20 June 1982) he showed an understanding of why Britain went to war. At the same time he urged magnanimity in victory. 'We don't honour the dead by being intransigent and vindictive. The enormous problem now facing our political leaders, and in a different way the new leaders in Argentina, is how to rise to the events and make them the basis of some genuine reconciliation. Politically this is not easy. The normal political assumption is that shed blood cries for vengeance. Men have died to free the Falklands, so it becomes politically very hard even to think of compromises which once might have been accepted gladly. Victory, so far from freeing us, can begin to close off the options; unless there is the greatness of spirit to see beyond the immediate euphoria of winning and the immediate pain of our losses.' His hope and prayers were for 'greatness of spirit', and church leaders would do best to help politicians embrace that spirit.

Earlier, in a letter to *The Times* (30 April 1982), Habgood acknowledged that,

> Britain's actions can be morally justified, though a final judgement may have to wait until the mistakes and omissions over many years are seen in a clearer light.
>
> The danger is, though, that once a war has started it acquires its own momentum and becomes its own justification. The scent of 'victory' distorts preception. We can already observe this happening, and our emotional involvement will become stronger if casualties begin to mount. A subtle process begins whereby putting the 'Great' back into Great Britain becomes an unacknowledged war aim.

He concluded his letter: 'All honour to those who risk their lives in the cause of peace, whether by fighting or by abstaining from fighting. But we must be careful not to glorify the fighting itself, or see it as anything other than evidence of human failure.'

Again, we see the sensitivity towards those who are faced with making decisions against a background of conflicting and complex interests. This approach is apparent in connection with the controversial report, *The Church and the Bomb: Nuclear Weapons and Christian Conscience* (1982). Habgood considered that the report represented Anglican sanity at its best as it gave expression to different points of view even if its conclusions were definite in one direction. Reviewing the report in the *Guardian* (18 October 1982), Habgood came quickly to the point: 'In my own view the moral argument against nuclear weapons is unanswerable, though it is worth noting that at one point it rests on a psychological and political judgement about the importance of the nuclear threshold. Once the threshold is crossed, the argument goes, there is no other clear stopping-place short of all-out nuclear war.' Having commended the report, Habgood added that he did not wholly agree with it. 'My hesitations concern the attempt to harness the thrust of the moral argument against nuclear weapons to the pragmatic, political argument against them.' It is easy to establish and to say that nuclear weapons are evil. 'What can actually be done about them, however, and what can make the world "better" in the sense of being safer, is not so obvious. I am not at all sure that the Church as a corporate body would be wise to identify itself too closely with a particular political programme. It is not that churches have no right to make political judgements. Sometimes they have to. In a case of this complexity the problem is that decision-making must depend on a host of subtle factors which those not directly engaged in the business of politics have difficulty in estimating.' He did not leave the matter quite as vague as that, and posed some imponderables.

> Crucial among these is Britain's relationship with America. What messages actually fly between Whitehall and Washington? One of the main unspoken reasons for wanting to maintain an independent British deterrent is uncertainty about long-term American intentions in Europe. Is the US actively trying to sell us Trident? If so, what are we to make of vigorous American arguments in the past against British retention of a nuclear capability? Now that the moral pressure against nuclear weapons is increasing,

would America fear moral isolation if it were forced to carry the whole of NATO's nuclear burden alone?

These were the tantalizing questions which should not be pre-empted by the Church using the moral authority of a Christian platform.

Another organization with which Habgood is associated is the Council for Arms Control. This is an independent research organization concerned with the dissemination of ideas and information on arms control, and disarmament issues. Basically concerned with education, it was set up in the early 1980s when the Campaign for Nuclear Disarmament was making a comeback, and was intended to provide an alternative way of taking arms control and disarmament seriously. It was concerned with the steadying hand of dispassionate analysis and sober presentation in contrast to the banners and slogans of CND. Although Habgood was a founder member and remains a Council member, he has not been really active in it, but his sympathies are with its aims and work. Fellow Council members include Conservative, Labour and Liberal MPs, military men and academics and people actively concerned with arms control at high levels.

Habgood is also one of the special advisers to the Foundation for International Conciliation. The other two advisers are Ambassador Rikhi Jalpal, former Ambassador to the Soviet Union and now Assistant Secretary-General of the United Nations, with special responsibility for the Committee on Disarmament; and Sir Anthony Parsons, who was the United Kingdom Permanent Representative to the United Nations 1979–82 and the Prime Minister's Adviser on Foreign Policy 1982–3. With trustees, a director and technical advisers, the Foundation, which was established in Geneva in 1984, is available to assist in critical situations in the world. When confrontation and deadlock seem to be the reflex responses to disputes and negotiations of national or international importance, there is urgent and obvious need to find another way, a different approach. The work of the Foundation is by stealth, and to look at its aims is to bask in a Habgoodian environment. I quote from a prospectus:

> A precedent has already been set for an alternative to current procedures. In the mid-1960s, three nations in South East Asia were at war, rejecting all proposals for negotiation or settlement through the United Nations or the International Court of Justice. Mediation was attempted by Premier Sato and Robert Kennedy, without success.
>
> Then a little-known group of academics, specializing in techniques of conflict-resolution, met in London with representatives of the three nations concerned. Working together over a period of months the parties in dispute made use of new techniques to analyse the conflict, gradually developing a lasting peace agreement.
>
> This success has never been publicized and subsequent uses of the techniques elsewhere have often been in strict confidence, so the procedures remain largely unrecognized for the promise they hold.
>
> Now this new approach is being offered in selected situations by the Foundation for International Conciliation. Some of the world's leading specialists in the field are being made available to advance the full range of related techniques, which together are called 'facilitation' . . . It is important to emphasize that, unlike the process of arbitration and judgement, the third party in facilitation has no power and never issues judgements or opinions. The specialist input is confined strictly to method. Thus no decisions are entrusted by the parties involved to anyone outside their control.

Because confidentiality is the strength of the Foundation, its work at any one time in any troubled area of the world is unlikely to be broadcast with a fanfare. But as 'truth is the daughter of time' so history may accord a number of success stories to the work of the Foundation.

Habgood's own 'facilitation' is likely to be more effective in national and international milieus than in his own Church, which appears to be suffering from a dose of law rather than love.

It is not only the big issues in which Habgood has an ethical interest. Others, of direct concern to many individuals, occupy much attention. Before looking at a few specific examples it is important to underline an irreversible plank in Habgood's thinking. He is ever cautious about using the Bible as a moral textbook. Many are the issues where the biblical teaching seems clear. Equally, interpretations change and deeper knowledge of some conditions can give moral judgements about them a new look. In a letter to *The Times* (4 September 1985) he writes: 'There is a factual and interpretative element in the making of actual moral decisions, which may well be ambiguous even when the moral principles themselves are clear. It is thus possible to hold, as I do, that innocent human life is sacred and must not be destroyed, while at the same time admitting a degree of uncertainty about the ethical significance of the earliest and most fragile stages of embryonic development.'

While recognizing that the law is a blunt instrument for dealing with intimate personal dilemmas, Habgood appreciates the need for law if society is going to remain sane. But there can be too much law.

A big issue of the 1960s was abortion, which led to the 1967 Act. Once the fundamental principle of respect for human life is invoked, any sense of perspective is washed away. Here, however, is an issue in which an acceptance that some abortions are morally allowable led to a situation in which it seemed as if almost any abortion could be justified. The liberal-minded person is trapped in a dilemma, for he is often wrongly accused of refusing to draw or recognize limits. If one looks closely at the issue there *are* limits, and Habgood drew them, writing in May 1974:

> The point is that any sacrifice of a human life (including that of a foetus) is an evil, but there may be very special circumstances when it is the lesser of two evils. Thus, in weighing the life of a young foetus against the health of its mother, it may reluctantly be decided that abortion is the lesser evil. But can we honestly believe that the equation is the same when what is at stake is not the health, but the happiness, the convenience or even the good name of the mother?

The John Corrie Abortion (Amendment) Bill aiming to stop abortion on demand and seeking stricter controls after twenty weeks, came before Parliament during 1979 and 1980. The Roman Catholic Church was very vocal in its support of the Bill, as were many Anglicans. Habgood spun a grenade into the debate, causing much ferment. In a letter to *The Times* (30 January 1980) he made it clear that there was another Christian view on the matter.

> All Christians, I imagine, deplore the need for abortion, and would see it in terms of a difficult choice between evils. But not all would subscribe to the simple belief that human life begins unequivocally at conception and from that moment must be accorded the rights of full personhood. There is an element of emotional blackmail in language which refers to the murder of thousands of babies, and I believe it is both unwise and unnecessary to polarize the discussion as if it were a question of murder on the one hand or the removal of what some call an insignificant piece of tissue on the other.
>
> A Church of England working party, whose report was one of the factors paving the way for the 1967 Act, refused to define the status of the fertilized ovum, on the grounds that any such definition would be arbitrary and inseparable from the moral judgements which it might then be used to justify.
>
> The more fully theologians try to come to terms with what is actually known about human development, the more sensible that refusal seems. The exchange of shrill certainties about a matter on which, in the nature of the case, certainty is impossible, only serves to make an agonizingly difficult problem more intractable.

Habgood advocated not further legislation but a code of practice which 'could remedy the proven abuses while allowing the flexibility which the practice of good medicine requires'.

Habgood's position is not an easy one. To hold that in most complex ethical fields it is probably more healthy to provide a stimulus for continuing broadly-based discussion than to settle prematurely into fixed positions requires dogged determination. Every pressure is to ease one into a polarized position.

In discussions on suffering and the love of God, there is a

traditional view that we need our weaker brethren – the crippled in mind, body or morals – to develop our attitudes of compassion and thus become spiritually refined. To many scientists, such a view seems of monumental and repulsive selfishness, and compassion alone would suggest that, however much a defective child may develop its parents' fortitude and consideration, its own courage and the onlooker's capacity to be moved to tears, yet it would be better had the child never been conceived and born. Problems raised by genetical prognoses and ethico-legal ones are clamouring for attention.

Inability to produce children can cause great unhappiness to a married couple. Medical techniques of relieving distress are far advanced. Artificial inseminination and *in vitro* fertilization have entered people's normal vocabulary. As a member of the Ethical Committee of the Medical Research Council Habgood was involved with producing guidelines on *in vitro* fertilization. He has lectured to the annual conferences of the London Medical Council and of Theatre Nurses. He is among those who are concerned about the consequences for society of creating a steadily widening gulf between the physical processes of reproduction and their normal emotional and personal concomitants. 'This is worrying, because the close link between the physical and the personal is a distinctive feature of our humanity. In simple terms, human beings should be conceived, and born, and brought up in love. The fact that this does not always happen is no reason for condoning gratuitious threats to the ideal.'

As the gap between what is technically possible and what is humanly desirable widens, Habgood's alarm increases. Ovum and sperm banks, frozen embryos, proxy parents are *here*. If science cannot be stopped, can it be controlled? Is science capable of self-discipline?

At the other end of life's spectrum the picture is no less gloomy. 'The Christian attitude towards death entails a readiness to let people die but an unwillingness actually to take life. The distinction between passive and active euthanasia, though a fine one, is therefore of fundamental importance. Doctors at present do their work successfully in areas where the distinction is blurred. If it were removed by legislation, the consequent changes in public attitudes are likely to be far greater than now envisaged.' Giving a Christian view of euthanasia at a conference of the Society of Health on 19 December 1973 (published in the *Royal Society of Health Journal*, June 1974), Habgood reminded his audience that in Christian thought death is both an end and a beginning. Death must be neither feared nor courted. 'Thus while Christians have glorified martyrs, and have seen the martyr's death as in some sense the apogee of faith, they have persistently abhorred suicide as the supreme instance of faithlessness.'

If death is not to be courted, are there not circumstances when it may be welcomed as a friend? This view underlay the 1965 report *Decisions about Life and Death* (Church of England Board for Social Responsibility) on which Habgood commented: 'Its authors argued persuasively for the view that patients who might otherwise be subjected to a battery of sophisticated medical techniques designed to preserve a bare minimum of life, ought to be allowed the right to die. It was recognized that particular decisions might be extremely difficult, but the general principle was clearly stated, namely "that in a given case, medical treatment should extend so far and no further".' Habgood supported this principle, while warning against the dangers of active euthanasia. He had been chilled by a remark made to R. M. Hare by a doctor, in connection with the proposal to allow euthanasia. It was overdrawn, but the point could not have been more forcefully made. The doctor said: 'We shall start by putting patients away because they are in intolerable pain and haven't long to live anyway; and we shall end up by putting them away because it's Friday night and we want to get away for the weekend' (*Personality and Science*).

Abortion legislation had shown that safeguards and assurances given when the Bill was passed had to a considerable extent been ignored. There was no reason for thinking that should legislation be enacted on euthanasia, the position would be different. 'Unrealistic feelings of uselessness, the desire not to be a nuisance, unwillingness to face the problems of old age, would all combine to put pressure on those who were reaching a stage in life when they were easily influenced to prefer a quick way out. Some might welcome this picture.

But for the Christian who sees death as God's final action in a human life, it is worth the effort of trying to maintain fine distinctions within our present practice, in order to prevent ourselves from creating such a society.'

Habgood is not a man with answers to the searching moral questions of our time. That is plain. But the words of the great Richard Hooker, when he warned that things which seem plain may be more plain than true, are worth recalling. If we approach Habgood's thought in this area from a new perspective, we see something quite different. Suddenly all is not problems and problem-solving but mystery and the mystery is that of the Kingdom of God. What do we find in this Kingdom? Habgood mentioned three aspects of it in a sermon at an international conference held at Maryknoll, New York, in August and September 1984.

> First, there is the positive experience of not knowing; the positive acceptance that not all problems have solutions, at least not solutions of the kind that emerge from rational analysis . . . There is a larger mystery surrounding us, and part of our vocation as Christians is to acknowledge that mystery; and not to be afraid of not knowing. Out of this not knowing can develop a new humility, a new flexibility, a new readiness – to use a phrase of Alan Geyer's – to rethink the unthinkable.
>
> A second, and closely related, area of learning is learning to live with failure. Part of the mystery of God's Kingdom is the mystery of failure, rejection, wastage, suffering, the seed on barren ground, Christ on the cross. To participate in it is to begin to lose the lust for success . . .
>
> A third element in the mystery of the Kingdom is the invulnerability of hope. If our lives are surrounded, not just by threatening darkness and agonizing dilemmas in which it is hard to contemplate the possibility of failure, but by a loving purpose bringing life out of death, then there is always hope.

It is something to keep hope alive in a troubled and scared world. Habgood strives to do this by being a passionate moderate and reconciling agent.

9

Firm Rock and Elastic Freedom

Habgood's ministry at St John's, Jedburgh from 1962 to 1967 was full but not completely fulfilling. Before the offer of Jedburgh there had been the possibility of appointment to St John's Princes Street, Edinburgh – an important and fashionable church. He was turned down by the Vestry. An appointment to this church would have had more than a taint of Kenneth Carey nepotism about it.

When he went to Jedburgh, Habgood resolved to remain there for five years, believing that no effective work of lasting worth can be accomplished under that length of time. Despite attractive offers during that period nothing was given consideration. Such unbending determination saves a lot of fuss and fret over 'invitations' of advancement. When his five years ended, what should he do? He did not see another parish as the next extension of his ministry. Neither did he think of remaining in Scotland. Absences from Jedburgh increased as he undertook lecturing, preaching and broadcasting engagements far afield, and membership of informal working groups involved many residental conferences. His name was becoming familiar if not yet widely known.

Jedburgh had given him valuable experience of working in a non-established Church where the cure of souls was limited to the gathered congregation. The contrast with England strengthened his growing conviction of the value of the Church of England's pastoral possibilities through being established, and it was later to lead to his advocacy of 'folk religion'.

Jedburgh was important for another reason. It was the place where three of his children, Laura, Francis and Ruth, were born. Adrian was born during the Birmingham years.

Habgood had met Rosalie Mary Anne Boston in Cambridge. Rosalie, an accomplished musician, was giving piano lessons at the Choir Schools of King's College and St John's College and violin lessons in some county primary schools. She went to a party at Westcott House. There she met the Vice-Principal, John Habgood, and that, in a manner of speaking, was that! It was love at first meeting. The phrase 'love at first *sight*' is not quite correct, for although she was faced with a gently impressive figure the reserved manner and clerical black carried a hint of celibacy. However, at their third meeting they became engaged and six months later, in 1961, they were married. A good friend and wise priest – to them and to countless others in the Church of England – Canon Frank Bennett, well known as Rector of Wigan, then Vicar of Maidstone and by 1961 Vicar of Minehead, officiated at the ceremony. At Jedburgh the roots of family life took firm hold and grew without too much extraneous disturbance. Habgood saw to that! Family life remains the precious, protected and sustaining area of his existence. In their own marriage the Habgoods combine idealism and realism and although his views have a slightly old-fashioned air about them they are none the worse for that.

After five years in Jedburgh, what should Habgood do? He favoured something with a teaching ingredient in it. In 1967, the Queen's College, Birmingham was looking for a new principal to succeed Arthur Stanley Gribble (principal since 1954) who was moving to Peterborough as a canon residentiary. For all kinds of reasons Queen's was at a low ebb and the number of students was small. Almost as soon as the five-year deadline had passed, Habgood was approached and asked to apply for the principalship of Queen's. He did so and was able to dictate the terms on which he went. The college needed invigorating and a new direction.

The College began its life in 1828 as the Royal School of Medicine and Surgery. In 1843 it received a charter from Queen Victoria and changed its name to Queen's College; and in 1849 it established a theological faculty, as well as faculties of arts, law, engineering and architecture. Its original benefactor had tied it strictly to the Church of England which was fatal in mid-nineteenth-century Birmingham with its virile non-conformity. After reorganization of the medical faculty and the foundation of the university, Queen's was closed in 1907. Although 'down', it was not 'out', for the bones stirred again in 1923 when it was transferred to its present site at Edgbaston. Eleven years later it broke with its medical past and concentrated entirely on the training of theological students, becoming a recognized theological college of the Church of England. Some rebuilding was done which included a dignified Byzantine chapel. Many liturgiologists visit the chapel, for with its 'period' free-standing altar it is said to mark the beginning in England of the modern liturgical movement. Further expansion took place in the 1960s.

On 25 May 1967 the Council of Queen's, under its President, the Bishop of Bradford (Michael Parker), appointed Habgood as Principal. He needed no persuasion to accept and started work at the beginning of the September term. The challenge facing Habgood was not merely that of reviving Queen's. Stephen Lloyd, a member of the College Council and later Vice-President of the Governing Body, writes:

> Before his appointment the Council of the College had become interested in the possibility of changing Queen's into an ecumenical college but had not taken any action. When he attended a meeting of the College Council on 19 July 1967 as Principal-Elect John Habgood reported that he had been in touch with the Principal of Handsworth [Methodist] College and at his first meeting with the Council as Principal on 24 October 1967 on his initiative a committee was appointed with himself as its chairman to consider the establishment of Queen's as an ecumenical college.
>
> The task was undertaken with energy. An interim report was made to the Council in February 1968 and on 25 May 1968 exactly a year after his selection as Principal and only seven months after its creation John Habgood submitted to the Council a long and comprehensive report from his committee recommending that Queen's should become an ecumenical college and that the report be submitted to the Methodist Conference the next year so that Handsworth

> College could be amalgamated with Queen's with effect from September 1970.
>
> The constitution of Queen's was sufficiently flexible for the membership of its Council to become ecumenical. The report was adopted by the Methodist Conference in the summer of 1969 and John Habgood's programme was carried out as intended. From September 1970 he was Principal of an ecumenical college.

The actual timetable is impressive although it must not be thought that the ecumenical college was born without birthpangs. Writing in the College Magazine (*Regina*, Trinity 1969), Habgood said: 'All denominations must be prepared to put their traditions in the melting-pot in order to create something genuinely appropriate for a new kind of community.' Roger Schutz, Prior of Taize, has written: 'There is no reconciliation without mutual renunciation. On the day of visible unity, it will still be necessary to die to a part of themselves. Unless the grain dies, can it bear fruit?' (*The Power of the Provisional*, 1969).

In some ways the Anglican had to die more than the Methodist, not least in the delicate matter of intercommunion. This applied to the staff as well as to the intake of students. Meeting for relaxed yet concentrated discussion at the holiday cottage of a staff member in Wales, the new Anglican and Methodist staff began to get to know each other and, as Habgood reflects, 'to laugh together: we even managed to climb a small mountain together, and celebrated communion together for the first time over the breakfast table. William Strawson, who had been the senior tutor of Handsworth Methodist College, celebrated and for only the second time in my life I received communion from a non-Anglican. We all felt that this was an important occasion, and I think that for the Methodists present it acted as a reassurance that their sacramental ministry really was accepted within the college.'

The full-time teaching staff of six, including Habgood, plus a bursar, brought with them experiences which blended and gifts that clashed. The Methodists William Strawson, Trevor Rowe and John Turner – had enjoyed rich circuit ministries. In addition William Strawson had been an RAF chaplain and John Turner a university chaplain. The Anglicans were Raymond Hammer, who had served as Professor of Christian Doctrine at St Paul's University, Tokyo; and Rupert Hoare who was a Canon-Theologian of Coventry Cathedral and had studied Marxism under Professor Gollwitzer in Berlin. The theological positions of these men were very different and their approach to pastoralia and other topics varied. This was to be expected. Habgood's task was to enable them to catch and share a common vision of the College's future. They had to become a team. How do you form a team while retaining the total individuality of each member of it? As principal and 'co-ordinator' – leader is not a word he would use without qualification – Habgood conveyed an authority which did not rely on bombast or threats or reputation but which proved itself by what it had to give.

Before the College was transformed into an ecumenical one, Habgood had already changed its spirit, temper and tempo. He lost no time in making changes. Miss Edith Barnes, who was Habgood's private secretary until 1971, mentions some of them:

> Previously discipline had been strict, although some relaxations had been made prior to his arrival, but he brought new ideas which included some radical changes. He encouraged self-discipline rather than 'compulsion from above' and, in return for this freedom, every member of the college had to join a group whose concern was with practical duties and also with the care and discipline of its members. Formal ways of address were relaxed and Christian names became the norm. Whereas previously the college had been male-dominated, he encouraged wives of married students to share in the life of the college where possible. Some temporary married accommodation was initially provided for a few families and later on during his time at Queen's, a block of flats and flatlets for married students was built.

The pattern of worship was radically revised and simplified and the curriculum was revised with considerable emphasis on frontier topics. Frontier theology starts not from the Scriptures or from history but from the world as it is now. Insights from the past are used to tackle contemporary problems in the secular terms in which they arise. Such an approach requires an acute critical faculty as well as the gift of discernment, otherwise the world not only dictates the agenda but secularizes the answers. Theological insights do not come without travail of thought.

With ecumenicity came a great element of risk. And with risk there is always the probability of suffering. Some people are more prepared for the one than for the other. But the Christian should welcome risk and not be frightened by it. The Christian lives by promise. The New Testament does not erase the Old Testament, neither is it its complete fulfilment. The New Testament expands the horizon of promise to the ultimate point at which God will be all in all.

Habgood, whether at Queen's or elsewhere, appears to convey both strength and weakness. There is total confidence in God and the perpetual insecurity of faith. There is the absent leader and the great enabler. There is the forceful innovator and the tentative reformer. Paradoxically, if you try to label one 'strength' and the other 'weakness' you may find the opposite, or more likely, that neither is accurate. Nevertheless, it points towards personality.

Habgood was able to do so much so quickly at Queen's because of his personality. In one of her novels (*The Public Image*, 1968), Muriel Spark says: 'What is personality but the effect one has on others? Life is all the achievement of an effect. Only the animals remain neutral.' What effect could a man who cannot be called a 'thrusting leader' have on a college? It requires a particular quality to see situations clearly and then to be able to discern an appropriate way for following a middle line that does not sacrifice anything of major importance. This is the glory of compromise, hard-fought and won, not the weakness of 'anything for a quiet life'.

It also required a man who would remain himself. Habgood did! John Turner offered a reflection after four years of ecumenism (*Regina*, March 1974): 'Here was a principal who superbly exemplified the virtues of his own Anglican tradition but was always hearing "echoes" coming from other cultural patterns and traditions and then subtly weaving them into the pattern of college life. He is a man who bridges the gulf between the so-called conservative and the so-called radical, for he is both, all that Sir Herbert Butterfield meant when he wrote in *Christianity and History* about the firm rock and the elastic freedom which are needed in the church of today.'

On 14 October 1970 the new Queen's was officially inaugurated, with representatives of all the major British Churches participating led by the Archbishop of Canterbury (Michael Ramsey) and the President of the Methodist Conference (R. E. Davies). If an ecumenical Queen's was going to work, two matters had to be settled: the government of the college and the worship. From the outset Habgood ensured that the community was held together and given direction partly by the sense of personal freedom and responsible commitment and partly by meetings which were skilfully directed towards this end. The staff met briefly each day and once a week for an afternoon. The whole community met once a week for informal debate presided over by a student, and once a week for a decision-making session.

Worship was difficult to organize. In its manward aspect, worship in a theological college has three main functions: to be the focus of community life and the main agent of spiritual formation; to provide experience of a living tradition of worship as it exists within the Church, and also of the ways in which the tradition is changing; and to give opportunities for practice to those who will themselves be leaders of worship. The community must be a eucharistic one, and this means intercommunion. It was in accord with Habgood's preference that attendance at worship would be voluntary except at the Sunday Eucharist and the Tuesday preaching service. Before the union of the two colleges took place, the only agreement about worship was that there should be a complete acceptance of ministries and of communicants at the Eucharist. The Sunday Eucharist alternated between an Anglican and a Methodist rite. The weekday Eucharist was celebrated alternately by an Anglican and a Methodist member of staff and was according to a new Queen's rite.

There were inevitable tensions. After a short period Habgood wrote:

> Our initial hopes were to find a balanced pattern which allowed everybody to feel that their characteristic style and emphasis was represented in most acts of worship. The work of the Joint Liturgical Commission seems to have been based on this sort of assumption. We soon discovered, however, that such a pattern satisfied nobody. We had ignored the fact that each tradition has its own inner integrity, and that this must not be destroyed within a compromise solution if the worship is to "feel right" to the participants. We have therefore moved steadily in the direction of greater variety, and are trying to provide a secure base of familiar worship for those who feel they need it, together with plenty of encouragement and opportunity to explore in other traditions, or create our own. One notable achievement has been the creation of our own communion rite, which is generally felt to be very satisfactory, and which seems to have anticipated some of the more recent ecumenical thinking on the subject.

It must not be thought that the worship passage was smooth. The sea was rough with storms of valid and invalid ministries, clouds full of alcoholic and non-alcoholic wine, lightning caused by a hanging sanctuary lamp. These issues had to be faced and Habgood as the ship's captain had to ensure that the ship so recently launched did not sink. A former student, Peter Baldwin, now a parish priest in the Durham diocese refers to a very real problem during the transformation from Church of England chrysalis to ecumenical butterfly.

> There were many from the old Queen's College who would not accept as valid the orders of the Methodist minister. Some were accustomed to a daily mass . . . the answer for my first year was to provide costs of transport to take this small group to a local church for a mass on the days when there was a Methodist celebrant . . . Naturally worship was often the topic of discussion at the weekly college meeting where John [Habgood] would allow any matter whatsoever to be discussed. Here was the great occasion where student power was at its best. There was a feeling that "we" were running the college, though because of the respect that

> John was held in by the college, his occasional input of wise words prevailed.
>
> It is John's ability to listen carefully to argument and then to be able in a few words to sum everything up and present a good solution that sets him up as a man of tremendous stature. Over and over again in my contacts with him, it is his ability to concentrate and listen, and then to see a way forward that makes him the leader that he is.

Seeing ways forward, pursuing them, aiming for reconcilable goals is very different from achieving them in a Church (of England) which says one thing and practises another. Thus it is noteworthy that what was achieved at Queen's in a short time is very considerable. After he left Queen's Habgood wrote of his time as Principal:

> We deliberately left many things undecided. Nobody knew what lessons there were to be learnt in an ecumenical college, and therefore our aim was to provide sufficiently flexible structures to enable us to make real discoveries. The insecurities, and sometimes the apparent shapelessness of the college, were the price which had to be paid for our faith that God was asking us to do a new thing. On the whole the Churches, at least through their official organs, are frightened of doing new things, and it is depressingly true that even many ordinands look primarily for safety and stability. But it is becoming very clear that the Church of the future is going to have to adapt itself to quite new conditions, and everything will depend on whether it does this in a spirit of adventure and faith, or in sullen alarm.

'Frightened of doing new things'! Habgood was still at Queen's when the Anglican Methodist Unity scheme failed for the second time in May 1972. At the special session of the General Synod the vote was 65.81 per cent for, thereby failing by 9.19 per cent to reach the required margin of 75 per cent (although the bishops' vote was 85 per cent). Habgood was distressed. Many students at Queen's were angry. It was a painful business for Anglicans like Habgood to learn how to be loyal to an organization when one deeply disagrees with what the organization has done. There was no mistaking his feelings. Preaching to the College, he said:

> The Church of England has lost its authority as an ecumenical pace-setter and bridge-builder.
>
> The bishops have lost a good measure of their authority as leaders; they tried to lead, perhaps too half-heartedly and too late, and their lead was rejected.
>
> Methodist leaders may well find themselves under criticism for having led their rank-and-file members up the garden path.
>
> Both Churches must have lost some of what little authority they have as agents of reconciliation in the world.

It was obvious that, following his experience at Queen's, Habgood would be a candidate for national ecumenical consultations. After the Anglican–Methodist fiasco it was clear that any idea of new 'schemes' for unity would remain frozen at the starting-post. Habgood admitted: 'The very word "scheme" implies some sort of blueprint, or perhaps a botched-up compromise, which everybody could feel as a threat to the integrity of their tradition. We have learnt our lesson.' These words were written in 1976, when the General Synod was about to debate the Ten Propositions of Unity which the Churches' Unity Commission had asked all the major denominations to respond to during 1977. In view of what follows, the Ten Propositions are worth recalling:

i We reaffirm our belief that the visible unity in life and mission of all Christ's people is the will of God.

ii We therefore declare our willingness to join in a covenant actively to seek that visible unity.

iii We believe that this search requires action both locally and nationally.

iv We agree to recognize, as from an accepted date, the communicant members in good standing of the other covenanting Churches as true members of the Body of Christ and welcome them to holy communion without condition.

v We agree that, as from an accepted date, initiation in the covenanting Churches shall be by mutually acceptable rites.

vi We agree to recognize, as from an accepted date, the ordained ministries of the other covenanting Churches, as true ministries of word and sacraments in the holy Catholic Church, and we agree that all subsequent ordinations to the ministries of the covenanting Churches shall be according to a common ordinal which will properly incorporate the episcopal, presbyterial and lay roles in ordination.

vii We agree within the fellowship of the covenanting Churches to respect the rights of conscience, and to continue to accord to all our members such freedom of thought and action as is consistent with the visible unity of the Church.

viii We agree to continue to give every possible encouragement to local ecumenical projects and to develop methods of decision-making in common.

ix We agree to explore such further steps as will be necessary to make more clearly visible the unity of Christ's people.

x We agree to remain in close fellowship and consultation with all the Churches represented in the Churches' Unity Commission.

The Church of England's green light to pursue a form of covenant with other Churches flashed at the General Synod on 10 July 1978, but there was an ominous number of clerical dissentient votes.

The notion of covenanting appealed to Habgood for, as he said, 'it implies commitment to a journey whose end is only distantly perceived; but it is a journey *together* . . . The idea is that a commitment to share can be made by any Churches that wish to do so, long before the legal and administrative tangles of complex organizational unity even begin to hove in sight.'

The Churches' Council for Covenanting was formed holding its first meeting on 24 November 1978 under the chairmanship of Bishop Kenneth Woollcombe. Participating Churches were the Church of England, the Methodist Church, the Moravian Church, the United Reformed Church and, a little later, the Churches of Christ, with consultants from other Churches. A year later Habgood joined the Council. He regarded the work of the Council as having a 'make or break character'. Writing in the 'Bishop's Letter' in January 1980, he said: 'It is only if we really care, only if we are prepared to relax our faces towards one another, that we have any hope of succeeding. But if we, who ought to have so much in common, fail when it comes to the crunch, what hope can we offer to a divided world?' Habgood had joined the Council in 1979 after Professor Douglas Jones left it. Jones had resigned over the Ordination of Women issue and realistically realized it was not worth going on. The Council needed a replacement which would be seen as a gesture of confidence in the Church of England's participation. Habgood, then Bishop of Durham, was that person.

The work of the Council was never less than stimulating. The Methodists bore the scars of yesteryear. The Moravians had bishops, but not in the apostolic succession as Anglicans knew it. Moravian bishops are representatives not rulers, and they are ordainers. The United Reformed Church had an innate fear of bishops. Bishops may preside at ordinations as a matter of good order, but not of faith. The doctrine of succession must not deny past ministries. The bishop must not be independent of, nor have, power to override councils.

The Church of England membership was bound to lead to a firework display for it included a rocket, sparklers, a volcano, Roman candles and a Catherine-wheel. Members included Christian Howard, David Brown (Bishop of Guildford), John Taylor (Bishop of St Albans) and Graham Leonard (then Bishop of Truro).

One of Habgood's written contributions, 'Episcopacy as a symbol', will be considered in the next chapter.

The report *Towards Visible Unity: Proposals for a Covenant* appeared in 1980. The covenant was intended to enable five Churches to work together more closely in mission, to share resources more effectively and to grow gradually into a deeper unity. It was not a union scheme, because each of the Churches would remain legally autonomous after the covenant. The heart of the report was the making of the covenant, set within an act of worship in which leaders from the Free Churches would be made bishops; priests or 'presbyters' from all the Churches would be ordained; acts of reconciliation would take place; and promises between the denominations could be exchanged.

All participating Churches, with the exception of the Church of England, unanimously signed the report. It can never have been a possibility that the Anglo-Catholics on the Council would be able to agree to anything that altered or diluted the catholic interpretation of the office of bishop. They objected principally to a provision allowing the United Reformed Church in particular a seven-year breathing space during which not all their leaders would have to become bishops. For the Anglo-Catholics this violated the basic Anglican commitment to the invariable rule and practice of episcopal ordination. To accept in effect as though they were bishops, ministers – for example, United Reformed Moderators – who have deliberately not been ordained as bishops, implied a wholly functional view of episcopacy and treated bishops as an expendable administrative convenience. This provision, which they said was argued for on theological grounds by the majority signatories and not as a kindly concession or a tolerable anomaly, constituted for the Anglo-Catholics a decisive flaw in the total proposals. There were other matters of concern too, such as women ministers, but the report appeared with a fifteen-page memorandum of dissent signed by Graham Leonard, Canon Peter Boulton and O. W. H. Clark.

Graham Leonard, by then Bishop of London, pointed out that the Church of England must make a clear distinction between *covenanting as a process*, which he believed could and should be supported, and the *content of the present proposals.* The substantial differences must be resolved, he wrote, 'in obedience to the truth, even if it takes time. In almost every reference to unity in the New Testament, it is associated with truth. In practice it is also necessary to avoid a situation in which, after covenanting, hopes of closer relations are not fulfilled because differences of understanding and practice, particularly with regard to the sacramental life of the Church and the role of the ordained priesthood, have not been faced . . . If our ministry is to be rooted in truth, the purpose of entering the covenant must not be to secure unity at any price but to come to a common mind as to what is "of God" in our present tradition and must be embodied in our new relationships.'

From 1980 to 1982 the report was thrown to the Churches for consideration. A polarized, polemical pamphlet war ensued in the Church of England. Habgood was active in speaking for the proposals in debate and discussion. He saw the exciting reasonableness of the covenant. Yet he knew in his heart that once again the Church of England was going to say 'No', and it did so in July 1982 at the General Synod when the House of Clergy ensured the covenant's defeat. Unity was dead in this or similar forms, perhaps for a generation.

As a result of the vote Habgood resigned as a member of the Churches' Council for Covenanting and wrote an article for *The Times* (13 July 1982) in which he saw, 'no escape from the bleakness of the immediate ecumenical outlook'. The Church of England had to do some heart-searching. 'A certain degree of defensiveness among those who see themselves as the guardians of a tradition is both understandable and right. But stubborn refusal to face threats to cherished beliefs and to live with internal tensions seems to point to something rather more seriously wrong.' He criticized the Council for Covenanting for making a serious mistake when, 'on the eve of publishing its proposals, it was presented with a substantial minority report. In deciding to stick to the timetable imposed by the synod, instead of trying yet again to resolve the difficulties, it ensured opposition from the very start. Thereafter, the procedural rigidity of the various Churches removed any subsequent possibility of re-negotiation.'

But Habgood must have known there was no possibility of changing the convictions (for that is what it would have meant) of the Anglo-Catholic trio. Ecumenical activities would continue, but unofficially at a local level. He concluded his article: 'Above all Anglicanism needs to improve its own theological understanding of itself. A bridge church must know its own mind if it is not to come apart every time it is tested.' The Lambeth Conference of 1988 will provide the opportunity of a thorough re-examination of the Anglican position.

Habgood's pleasanter ecumenical encounters come through the British Council of Churches (BCC) of which he is a leading member. The BCC, like the World Council of Churches, suffers from constant misunderstanding and occasional abuse. Reports proliferate from individual churches on identical topics where the issues would be better considered under the auspices of the BCC drawing members from all churches. Habgood is a critic of the Church of England in this regard: it tends to ignore the BCC whereas the World Council of Churches exists on another planet not to be visited. Yet it is the BCC which is bringing church leaders together. The Archbishop of Canterbury (Robert Runcie) is President of the BCC but he has decided to concentrate on the Anglican Communion, leaving his archiepiscopal counterpart at York to be the chief Anglican presence at the BCC – and in Geneva too. The arrangement suits each archbishop. The issues at the BCC and the WCC tend to be less ecclesiastical.

As the western cultural framework begins to strain to breaking-point, this framework, within which most of our contemporary political, social, economic and religious questions are but symptoms of a deeper failure, forces itself high on the agenda of ecumenical councils. They need a contribution which combines very sharp insight and encourages stability. Habgood fits this role, and he is well regarded at the BCC and the WCC by not being a 'party' man. Philip Morgan, BCC General Secretary, writes:

In the view of many, the growth of pressure groups within

> the Church of England is not helpful in determining the mind of that Church. Bishop Habgood is a man of precise thoughtful opinion supported by clear and resolute conviction and is not tied to a popular line or given to allying himself with the enthusiasms of the hour. His familiarity with both scientific and theological disciplines gives him an objectivity which is particularly valuable.
>
> His academic distinction, intellectual honesty and clarity of thought and speech, supported by obvious Christian commitment and personal integrity, make him of great personal stature. Those who suggest a degree of detachment both fail to recognize the value of this in a very confusing world and have not taken the trouble to get near enough to the man to discover his personal warmth.

A tremendous fillip to the BCC was, ironically, the visit of Pope John Paul II to Britain in 1982. (The Roman Catholic Church is not a member of the BCC.) With the constant support of Cardinal Basil Hume and delicate negotiations, representatives of the BCC met the Pope in the Deanery of Canterbury on 29 May 1982 and shared in conversation and a meal. The Pope invited some BCC members to visit Rome. This was more than a thaw. The ice had broken and the sun was beginning to warm the water. So a group of twelve British church leaders appointed by the BCC and the (RC) Bishops' Conferences of England and Wales and Scotland went to Rome from 26 to 29 April 1983. They were, from the BCC besides Habgood, Martin Conway, C of E, Secretary for Ecumenical Affairs of the BCC; Martin Cressey, United Reformed Church, Westminster College, Cambridge; Kenneth Greet, Methodist Church, Secretary of the Methodist Conference; Alastair Haggart, Scottish Episcopal Church, Bishop of Edinburgh and Primus; Philip Morgan, United Reformed Church, General Secretary of the BCC; and Elizabeth Templeton, Church of Scotland, theologian and writer. The Roman Catholic contingent comprised Alan Clark, Bishop of East Anglia; Cormac Murphy O'Connor, Bishop of Arundel and Brighton; Michael Richards, Heythrop College, London; James Quinn, Secretary of the Christian

Unity Commission of the Episcopal Conference of Scotland; and Francis Thomson, Bishop of Motherwell.

Most of the conversations were held in the Secretariat for Promoting Christian Unity. Among those taking part in the talks were Unity Secretariat officials: the President, Cardinal Johannes Willebrands; the Vice-President, Bishop Ramon Torella, who was shortly to leave to take up his appointment as Archbishop of Tarragona in Spain; the new Secretary, Father Duprey; and Mgr Richard Stewart. There were other meetings, not least with Cardinal Joseph Ratzinger, Prefect of the Sacred Congregation for the Doctrine of the Faith. Ratzinger and Habgood should have got on well together, for there is a similarity in certain layers of their thinking. There was a meeting with the Pope too.

Preparation for the meetings had been thorough on each side. The agreed subjects for discussion were peace; marriage discipline; dialogue with other faiths; faith and its reception; the spirituality of the Ecumenical Movement; and Councils of Churches as instruments of unity. Preparatory papers had been written and discussion was sensitive, but to the point. Marriage discipline – the cause of so much pain – occupied a full day, and on the group's return Habgood wrote of their discussions on this subject in a booklet *Rome '83: Returning the Pope's Visit*. The subject is stripped to essentials. What is the basis on which it is possible to claim that a marriage is Christian? Where can agreement between the Churches start? Has language as well as tradition got in the way of understanding? Following discussions with the Pontifical Council for the Family, it became clear to Habgood and the group that Rome accepts that 'it is not Catholic rites which ensure that a marriage is Christian, however desirable such rites might be; nor is it these which make it Catholic. The basis of marriage in Roman Catholic eyes is the same as that accepted by other Christians and enshrined in British law, namely mutual consent to form a permanent and exclusive bond. And it is baptism, nothing more, which makes such a marriage Christian and Catholic.' If that is the case why, then, the Roman attitude towards mixed marriages, where the promises required of Roman Catholic partners are still a source of friction? What of the question of communion in interchurch families? 'For Roman Catholics the theology of the Church and sacraments is at stake in proposals to allow the non-Catholic partner in a marriage to receive communion at a Roman Catholic Mass, and even if ways were to be found of permitting this on special occasions, there would still be no possibility of reciprocating it.' It is a question which was raised and will be continually raised by non-Roman Catholic Churches. Habgood puts the point pungently: 'Their need [interchurch marriages] is made all the greater by the pressures of the modern world against Christian ideals of marriage, and by the dangers of indifferentism if the churches fail to hear their plea.' Habgood sensed a greater sensitivity on marriage discipline. Results are likely to be far off but, as he says, 'it would be faithless not to entertain some real hopes'. The scope for co-operation is more limited on such topics as contraception and abortion.

If this is the first of a series of meetings in Rome, then there are real signs of hope for progress on all kinds of matters.

The Curia still gave the BCC members the impression of great power, but its Cardinal members are having to respond to the world for they can no longer dictate to it. Perhaps here there is a quiet reformation taking place. Habgood is not one to look for easy or quick change from Rome – perhaps not much of a pace in his lifetime. But Rome is on the move, however slowly and cautiously. Writing in *Rome '83*, Alastair Haggart says: 'We need patience, mutual trust and encouragement; we need to *humanize* our ecumenical relationships.' The visit was a good beginning in this process. Alastair Haggart ended his article by quoting a few lines from 'A Sleep of Prisoners' by Christopher Fry:

The frozen misery
Of centuries, breaks, cracks, begins to move;
The thunder is the thunder of the floes,
The thaw, the flood, the upstart Spring.

Back in England the momentum continued. On 11 January 1984 the Roman Catholic bishops of England and Wales invited the leaders of other Churches to join them in conference for joint reflection and deliberation on the topic 'The Catholic Church and Church unity – present position and future plans'. Then the Archbishop of Canterbury and Cardinal Hume jointly invited a group of church leaders to spend three days together at Canterbury in April 1984. A major conference is planned for 1987.

This *is* 'the upstart Spring'. Habgood sees it as a form of discovery, of stripping and cleansing. It is bound to be painful in parts. At the Canterbury gathering he preached at an Anglican Eucharist celebrated by the Archbishop of Canterbury and attended by all the church leaders present. He reminded his fellow church leaders that they could not escape the implications of power. 'Yet all the time there has to be that nagging thought, that bell tolling in the back of our minds – "That is not the way with you". As in blind Bartimaeus, vision has to start with a plea for mercy. The marriage between privileges and duties, between claims and obligations, between dignities and burdens, has to begin here at the foot of the cross.' As with individuals, so with Churches.

> What scope is there, within our ecumenical concern, for taking much more seriously the possibilities of serving one another as Churches? Have we really got out of our systems, as Churches, the desire to lord it over one another? And the corresponding fear that we may in turn be lorded over?
>
> Please God we are long past quarrelling over who is the greatest. But how far have we actually gone in serving one another, and how far can we avoid the dangers of patronizing one another? Perhaps the clue lies in offering the distinctive gifts and grace Christ has given us in each of our traditions, not as if they were our possession, but as the mark of our nothingness, of our utter dependence on him.
>
> What have we that we have not received? And how can we truly possess it without giving it? And to whom can we give it except to the one who gave himself for us, and who calls us to be one body? Mutual service is a glorious possibility because it is in giving that we receive. It is in pardoning that we are pardoned. It is in dying that we are born to life eternal.

As a result of the visit to Rome, the 'Not strangers but pilgrims' process was started and Habgood was appointed chairman. All the major Christian Churches in Britain (including the Roman Catholic Church) were involved in this inter-Church process on the nature and purpose of the Church in the light of its mission. This bland description does no justice to one of the most exciting developments in the Churches for many a decade. During Lent 1986 the Churches embarked on what was called 'a unique process of prayer, reflection and debate in an attempt to discover how God wants us to work together in the years ahead'. Again, that sounds safe ecclesiastical jargon for doing nothing! But with the help of local radio it was not long before a great many people were first talking about and then participating in 'What on earth is the Church for?' In inner city areas and rural villages, in house groups and public bars Christians were meeting and discovering that what they shared was greater than what divided them. There was also pain and fierce disagreement – and honesty. In place after place a new spirit of enlightened commitment and co-operative endeavour became evident. Groups have continued to meet, and after discovering 'what on earth the Church is for' have started deepening their pledge to their local communities (God's world). It is of little use Christians saying they are the Body of Christ, if their presence in the community is conspicuously elusive. All kinds of local initiatives between the Churches, some more 'legal' than others, are taking place.

There are to be 'Not strangers but pilgrims' conferences during 1987 and the possibility of another nationally co-ordinated Lent course in 1988. Habgood sees all this as a broad-based attempt to get something of the spirit of the ARCIC conversations (with which he is not directly involved) into the practical business of ecumenical co-operation.

In his meeting with other Churches, Habgood revealed his own vision. It is one which he articulated in a sermon in York Minster (21 January 1984) in the presence of Cardinal Danneels, Archbishop of Malines-Brussels, to commemorate the fiftieth anniversary of the death of Charles Lindley Wood, 2nd Viscount Halifax, who himself was a man of vision. The vision was of parallel Churches, in full communion with one another, united in faith and in common allegiance, yet preserving their own identity.

This vision remains in my view an essential half-way house on the road to full and complete unity.

I have always been a believer in unity by stages. The stage of parallel existence can be criticized as administratively untidy and theologically anomalous. Parallel episcopates in the same way would seem to mock the basic idea of episcopacy. It is clear that a stage of close, but not yet complete, interrelationship between Churches should not be allowed to continue indefinitely. But the essential thing which such an intermediate stage would allow is time for people to grow together, time for trust and mutual understanding to develop, time to explore one another's traditions within a framework of commitment and communion. Without commitment to one another, there can be no real growth. With too much commitment demanded too quickly, the problems of identity loom too large. The vision, all those years ago, of some kind of uniate relationship, may be impossible as it was then conceived. But in principle it was a wise one.

The growing relationship between the Church of England and the Roman Catholic Church is one of the most remarkable features of the ecumenical scene. Even twenty years ago, who would have thought it possible that the English Roman Catholic Cardinal of Westminster and the Archbishop of York would walk together through the streets of York to a service at York Minster to mark the four-hundreth anniversary of the death of Margaret Clitheroe? That is what happened on 31 March 1986. In his sermon Habgood held that religion is dangerous stuff and the memories of the past are still with us.

Historically speaking, one of the reasons for today's indifference to religion in countries where religious persecution once reigned, is precisely this frightening vision of what religious enthusiasm can do. We are still paying for the fires and the hangings and the crushings of four centuries ago. And on a lesser scale we go on paying for our divisions, and for the aura of petty religious squabbling which still wafts around us in the public imagination. It is not for nothing that 'couldn't care less' is perhaps the most deadly disease in our modern society.

But it provides no real answer. To possess no deep springs of emotion, no idealism, nothing we really care about, nothing to live and die for, is to lose half of our humanity. It is to create a dangerous vacuum into which all kinds of secular fanaticisms can pour. The modern world makes its martyrs – secular ones – with no less brutality than the world of Margaret Clitheroe.

Religion won't in the end go away. And the question is how to live with this dangerous reality, how to cope with this paradox of religious impulses which can rise to such heights and fall to such terrible depths?

Habgood's work with the BCC and the WCC takes him to many countries where he sees the paradox at its sharpest points. For example, he was one of a seven-person delegation visiting Lebanon, Syria, Jordan, Israel and the territories of the West Bank, Gaza and East Jerusalem, and Egypt during September 1981. (The report, published in 1982, was *Towards Understanding the Arab-Israeli Conflict.*) He went to Argentina in 1985 with the WCC and attended a Church Leaders' Meeting in Harare in December 1985 when the subject was South Africa. The travels are likely to increase in frequency and duration for he is much involved in the work of the Church and Society unit of the WCC.

He was also a member of a small BCC working party which tried to think in a far-reaching way about some of the changes taking place in our society. The thoughts of this '1984 Group' were crystallized in the popular book *The Other Side of 1984* by Lesslie Newbigin. We will consider some of these shortly.

Here it is sufficient to pause and remember that in all Habgood does, a key word is reconciliation – or 'the healing of memories' as he likes to call it. On his bookshelves are four volumes by Karl Barth on *The Doctrine of Reconciliation*, comprising some 2,600 pages in all. Barth says: 'Reconciliation is the restitution, the resumption of a fellowship which once existed but was then threatened by dissolution. It is the maintaining, restoring and upholding of that fellowship in the face of an element which disturbs and disrupts and breaks it . . .' Habgood says:

> Reconciliation, whether in the political sphere, or in industrial relationships, or between Churches, may be more complex and messy than reconciliation between individuals. It may be less easy to apply the direct message of the cross of Christ to the way corporate bodies, like nations and unions, behave than to individual sinners. But the basic principles are the same. There can be no reconciliation without the pain of bearing wrong; no reconciliation without a kind of incarnation, a putting oneself in the shoes of the other person; no reconciliation without faith to see beyond the obstacles, hope to cling to some distant goal, and love to motivate the process.

10

Symbol and Function

While he was at Queen's College, Habgood wrote a short essay on the subject of authority. He distinguished between extrinsic and intrinsic authority in this way: 'A man's extrinsic authority is that which he has by virtue of his office. A policeman's authority is extrinsic in that it does not depend ultimately upon his personal strength or virtue or any other abilities, but on the fact that he has been designated by society, as a policeman. His personal qualities are not irrelevant to the fact that he has been so designated, but they are not the basis of his authority, which is something given to him, not inherent in him.

> Intrinsic authority, on the other hand, belongs to a person as such. Somebody is accepted as having this kind of authority when he has made himself an expert, when it is clear that he really knows what he is saying or doing, irrespective of what office he holds. Such authority is concerned more with stature than with status.
>
> Most actual authority contains both elements in varying degrees. To have to rely too heavily on extrinsic authority is to find oneself in the classic authoritarian dilemma; there is an inevitable pressure towards defensiveness, rigidity, overbearingness and pomposity. To be at the opposite extreme, however, to have intrinsic authority without status is to be equally under pressure. It may be the pressure of frustration, the pressure of finding oneself a threat to others, or the more subtle pressure of trying to make everything personal without the safeguards of officialdom. The man who becomes his own executioner in the pursuit of justice has taken intrinsic authority to its logical conclusion.

Holding these two aspects of authority in equilibrium is always challenging, never easy. Anyone who is called to, or seeks, a position of leadership is particularly prone to getting one or the other of them out of balance. Usually leadership is associated with power or rule. In the Church it is otherwise. No man with any semblance of sanity would deliberately seek high office in the Church. After all, there is no power in the office of bishop and a confused notion of what constitutes authority in the office he holds. Furthermore, the concept of the leader as also a servant must seem absurd to the onlooker. It is rather like being czar and commissar.

What is leadership? Mere prominence, which may owe nothing to personal quality or exertion, can hardly deserve the name. Success is not the correct word. Indeed, it may be the negation of leadership. In the articulated bureaucracies of our modern State the road to official preferment seems to be most often trodden by those who combine a high level of capacity with a comparatively low standard of individuality. Is the bureaucratic tendency infiltrating the Church?

Again, neither knowledge nor what is often mistaken for knowledge, learning, is an essential constituent of leadership; yet all leaders should have some and want more.

Perhaps we near the mark when individual character and particular gifts, both natural and acquired, are fused. It is the union of dedication and ability.

We are not concerned for the moment with the way in which Habgood exercises episcope, but rather to look at the ever-changing pattern and expectations surrounding the office at the time of his nomination. One of the emphases brought out at the 1968 Lambeth Conference was, 'Simplicity in life, humility in manner, and joy in serving should be the marks of a bishop's life.' It has become something of a neurosis, though at the time it may have needed emphasizing. It is linked with the word 'servant'. The Church of England has for some time been falling over backwards to prove its servant worth. It is doing so before it has considered all the consequences which follow on being a servant Church. A bishop may suffer from sanctified exhaustion after a hectic week trying his best to be serviceable. Here is the rub. A bishop is pressed, pestered and persuaded for his views on subjects ranging from cabaret clubs to test-tube babies and the whole range of ecclesiastical activity from gargoyles, graveyards and garden parties to questions of vesture and gesture in church: all this on top of the physical activity to which he is subjected. But a bishop cannot have, and is not meant to have, a considered view or even a view at all on everything and to be everywhere. A bishop can *serve* all but not *service* all. That is why there should be a shared, and constitutionally shared, ministry with his senior diocesan staff. Somewhere, someone will have an answer. On the other hand, episcopal government and constitutional government are not natural partners and are not meant to be.

Any priest called to the office of bishop must have agonizing thoughts rushing through his mind when the formal letter from No 10 Downing Street arrives. Will his *natural* gifts be neglected or abused? Will he become little more than a purple-bibbed bureaucrat? If he is to stoke the spiritual fires of clergy, how can he ensure his own are not neglected? He knows his history and has seen how high office can have a vacillating effect upon its holder. It may enable or disable. How can he be sure that he, as a person, does not decrease as the Crockford entry increases?

The Church of England includes various expressions of common loyalty. The bishop is a focus of unity. The much and wrongly derided *via media* of Anglicanism has special responsibilities for the bishop. He is neither advocate nor judge, prelate nor pawn, but he has a reconciling function. Many people hold the view that the attempt to conflate incompatibles is wrong because it seeks to neutralize ideas or even people. It would be wrong if it sought to neutralize, but it does not. The reconciling bishop probes, penetrates and prays with issues, or people, until the shell of prejudice or misunderstanding falls away and the kernel is reached. (I do not say it is the function of the episcopate to crack nuts!) Obstacles may be circumvented but principles are always faced by the true reconciler.

Another way, and a good one, in which the work of the bishop is changing concerns his attendance at public worship. We are still slow to think of the bishop as the President of the Eucharist. Too often he is merely a part of the finale brought on at the end to give a blessing just before the final curtain. Bishops ought to be curtain raisers, and nowhere better than when celebrating the Eucharist.

A church building should not be a place where reality loses its sting on the way through the door, a place where the 'sacrament' of disengagement is celebrated. It is important that people take with them into church their imperishable problems and nattering neuroses and heartbreaks and, equally important, their overwhelming joys and gaiety and happiness. There is a *man* under every mitre, with his own problems, needs and temptations as well as joys. *He* needs support too.

In any bishop's part in the hurly-burly of church life today, there is need for a theological grip on the stewardship of time. Above all, this requires the ability to say 'No' and mean it. Ian Thomas Ramsey, perhaps the most influential, widely known and respected bishop of the latter half of the 1960s, could not or would not say 'No'. His death on 6 October 1972, at the age of only fifty-seven, when Bishop of Durham, was tragic and a shiver went through the Church of England. Just before his death he had prepared a paper for the Archbishop's Commission on Doctrine. This was its characteristic conclusion:

> I see two features as definitive of my approach to the Christian faith:
>
> 1 The notion of disclosure situations which impress and haunt; moments of vision, flashes of insight, contextualized silences.
>
> 2 The notion of theological exploration both in discourse and community structure. Authority belongs primarily to the vision; and when it is translated into discourse, interpretations, community structures and so on, these cannot have the givenness of God, the finality of the controlling vision itself. We must then distinguish between the Norm which is decisive for our commitment and derivative norms of which there are a multiplicity, and which need to be brought together in any particular Christian judgement, whether in doctrine or morality. It is for this reason that I relish the Anglican concept of a multiple Authority whose

> only unity and coherence is in the activity of God in Christ, which eludes any and all of the multiple expressions. Hence, the Anglican tradition can properly combine discipline and freedom, order and liberty, dogma and reason, discipline and a good conscience.

These marks of Anglican counterpoise were in some danger of being neglected. The times were against them. Polarization was the developing trend.

The appointment of Ian Ramsey's successor to the important see of Durham was awaited with much interest. The competing claims of the diocese and the national Church had to be considered. Durham wanted to see more of its bishop and hoped he would be a good administrator, sorting out administrative chaos. The wider Church wanted a man of distinction bringing fresh gifts to the corporate bench of bishops. In February 1973 the appointment was announced: that of John Habgood. He was consecrated on the Feast of St Philip and St James, 1 May, in York Minster and a little bit of history was made when the preacher was a Methodist minister, Habgood's staff member at Queen's, John Turner. He too mentioned that a bishop must learn to say 'No'. 'He must be given time to think, to read, to pray, lest he become a "dried-up orange".' He also warned against 'the man imprisoned in the Church, who can subtly come to think of God as the head of the clerical profession rather than "Head of Whole Mankind".'

Habgood has always had a reasonably realistic appreciation of his gifts as well as of his deficiencies. He once described one of his famous Durham predecessors, Bishop Joseph Butler, who was something of a hero of his, as 'a man of integrity, a man of balance and a man who was admirably down-to-earth in his understanding of the complexities of actual human nature'. Is that how Habgood sees himself?

It was over the tomb of another predecessor, Thomas Hatfield, that Habgood was enthroned as bishop in what is said to be the highest throne in Christendom. There, on 19 May 1973, Habgood began his episcopate committed to point people to God and taking as his text 1 Corinthians 2:2, 'I determined not to know anything among you save Jesus Christ and him crucified'. He stressed:

> There can be no evading the cost. To live with opposites, not in weak compromise, but constantly allowing different convictions, different emphases, different insights to react fruitfully on each other, entails a kind of death. We have to let others be themselves. If need be, we have to let them wound us. We have to reject utterly the sort of touchiness and pettiness and narrow-mindedness which can so quickly make us all scurry away from one another behind our defences. We have to bear the pain of difference if we are to know the joy of discovery.

Habgood believes it is in the tension between opposing emphases that Christian liveliness is to be found. That is why he is concerned about the intellectual crises which frequently occur in the Church – concerned but not afraid. He searches for truth but is not disappointed by its elusiveness. He is open to challenge but not a slave to any fashion or movement. Above all, he is serene because these are the only conditions under which faith can be exercised.

Addressing his first Diocesan Synod (23 June 1973) he quoted a well-known prayer that had come to mean a great deal to him. In a few words it is a pungent summary of his aims; its satisfactory fulfilment would be a fitting epitaph:

> O God, grant me the serenity to accept the things
> I cannot change, courage to change the things I
> can, and the wisdom to know the difference.

In most of what follows, whether exposition or critical analysis, Habgood will be writing and speaking as a bishop, yet still himself! It is necessary to understand his thinking on 'Episcopacy as a symbol' (the title of an unpublished paper to the Churches' Council for Covenanting) if one is to get any feeling about his gathering episcopate or make any sense out of his words. In his paper he wrote:

> The ordained ministry is both symbolic and functional. Both aspects are related to one another, but they also need to be distinguished.

In the document before us [at the Council] episcopacy is commended on functional grounds, the heart of the argument being that certain necessary functions in the Church can best be performed within the ministry of a single, identifiable and permanently designated person. The argument is open to question on historical grounds, and has to meet the criticism that in certain times and places the functions have been performed much better in other ways. Within my own experience of episcopacy [after six years of it] the symbolic aspects of the role are much the most important. They have to be combined with reasonably efficient performance of the functions expected of a bishop, but the fact that it is the bishop who is doing them counts for much more than the way they are done. For example, an episcopal visit to a parish is an occasion for that parish, a boost to morale, a reminder of the wider context in which its work is done, not because the bishop is wiser or more eloquent or more travelled than the local clergyman, though it is a help if he is all these things. What matters is that he symbolizes the relationship of the parish to the whole Church, and the Church to the givenness of the gospel. It is in this sense that his visit can be a means of grace.

Symbols depend on long associations and can arouse deep emotions – both sympathetic and antipathetic. They tend to be more stable than the functions through which their meaning is expressed. Episcopal functions are being subtly modified all the time, not least by synodical government. Episcopacy as a symbol, on the other hand, has remained relatively constant. Continuity is of its essence, not because some mysterious power has to be passed from generation to generation, but because it is destroyed as a symbol of the continuity of the Church if the means by which its continuity is preserved are disregarded.

Similarly, bishops are symbols of orthodoxy, and thus corporately have some residual functions as guardians of the faith, not because they are cleverer than other Christians or better educated theologically, but because being in communion with the bishop symbolizes an orthodox relationship with the remainder of the faithful. In other words, this is an extension of the bishop's role as the symbol of unity. The fact that all the faithful at some point in their lives, i.e. confirmation, come into direct contact with their bishop, reinforces his symbolic role as a touchstone of orthodox membership.

Those for whom this symbol is powerful fight for it intransigently, because its power depends on preserving it intact. Those who see episcopacy primarily in functional terms have no difficulty in giving or taking a little bit here and there, because functions are always changing anyway. The difference provides fruitful ground for misunderstanding.

If there can be broad agreement between Churches on a functional level, which seems not impossible, then the next, and much harder task, is to accept and appreciate one another's symbols. The frank recognition that they are symbols, not theological absolutes, would be an enormous step forward. Different sets of symbols do not necessarily have to be combined logically, as functions have to be. There may therefore be scope for a rich interweaving of symbols, which preserves their integrity while allowing scope for differences of emphasis.

Two further observations on symbol and function carry their own interest. Each illuminates something Habgood feels is important and in turn each offers a mirror image of Habgood – different but the same. First, in *The Power of Symbols* (1986) F. W. Dillistone shows how symbolic expression is the way to creative freedom.

I do not underestimate the importance of ordered structures or of signs which carry a uniform interpretation to all the members of a particular society. But human experience has shown that there is always the danger that a system of order, a framework of unambiguous signs, will become ends in themselves to be rigidly imposed and preserved from any possible deviation. In contrast to all forms of totalitarianism, the symbol stands for openness, for pointing towards alternative possibilities, for readiness to experiment in the hope of gaining a fuller understanding of reality. All this is summed up for me (by) Thomas Mann – 'To live symbolically spells true freedom'.

Secondly, in reviewing the book *How Brave a New World: Dilemmas in Bioethics* by Richard A. McCormick SJ (1981) in *Theology*, July 1982, Habgood quotes with approval a paragraph on bishops: 'Bishops should be conservative, in the best sense of that word. They should not endorse every fad, or even every theological theory. They should "conserve" but to do so in a way that fosters faith, they must be vulnerably open and deeply involved in a process of creative and critical absorption. In some, perhaps increasingly many instances, they must take risks, the risks of being tentative or even quite uncertain and above all being reliant on others in a complex world. Such a process of clarification and settling takes time, patience and courage. Its greatest enemy is ideology, the comfort of being clear, and above all the posture of pure defence of received formations.'

On the one side is openness and adventure; on the other side is conservation and tentativeness. Habgood holds these apparently contradictory traits in paradoxical tension. They are as inherent in the man as in the way he sees the office he holds.

The paradoxes are encapsulated in the particular bishopric of Durham. A bishop of Durham is marked off from his episcopal colleagues by some honorific distinctions which arouse curiosity and challenge explanation. He takes rank next to the Bishop of London. He is one of the three bishops who sit in the House of Lords by title of their sees, not in the order of their own consecration. In his official documents he uses a style commonly distinctive of archbishops, writing himself bishop 'by Divine providence', not, as is usual, 'by Divine permission'. The mitre which surmounts the arms of the see is bound with a ducal coronet; and he has the privilege of supporting the sovereign on the right side at a coronation. These honorific distinctions may be regarded as the last surviving relics of the splendour of the Palatine Jurisdiction which the BBBishop of Durham, alone among the bishops of England, once possessed, and which survived the changes and chances of history until 1836.

Perhaps more than any other bishopric in the country Durham has had a succession of strong and remarkable men – builders, governors, diplomatists, statesmen, warriors, scholars. Sumptuous feudal prelates could challenge kings. Outstanding figures of national history occupied 'The Bishoprick': men such as Ranulf Flambard (1099–1133), Hugh de Pudsey (1153–97), Anthony Bek (1284–1311), Richard de Bury (1333–45), Thomas de Hatfield (1345–82), Richard Foxe (1494–1502), Thomas Ruthall (1509–23), Cuthbert Tunstall (1530–61), Thomas Morton (1632–60) and John Cosin (1660–74).

It is well to remembr that there were bishops of Lindisfarne, of Hexham and of Chester-le-Street before there was a bishop of Durham. Aidan (of Lindisfarne) starts the list (635–51) and Cuthbert (685–8) was soon to follow. The history of saints is a puzzling exercise and presents an insoluble problem. Why should such vast influences have been wielded by such persons? How far does legend magnify the facts? A case in point is Cuthbert. Did his undoubted fame reflect rather the interest of a Church than the merits of an individual? It has been written of him: 'His life was one of asceticism rather than of labour. By far the larger part of it was devoted to the care of his own soul, and he was not remarkable either as a reformer of ecclesiastical order, or as a preacher of the Gospel. Yet the Church held him in extraordinary veneration.'

Habgood was successor to such men as these as well as Joseph Butler (1750–52), Shute Barrington (1791–1826) and William van Mildert (1826–36); and, nearer his own time, Joseph Barber Lightfoot (1879–90), Brooke Foss Westcott (1890–1901) and Herbert Hensley Henson (1920–39), men of character, learning and high distinction. If any contemporary bishop is thinking of ignoring this episcopal sweep of history, Auckland Castle, home of the bishops of Durham, is a healthy corrective. Although much of it is now used for diocesan offices, there is no disguising its grandeur. Bishops of Durham no longer rule by the sword, as some of them did. In fact they do not rule at all, but the sense of history is omnipresent whether at worship in the exceedingly imposing chapel or walking through State rooms where portraits of predecessors greet them. Habgood would not say, as one of his predecessors did, that 'history is a cordial for drooping spirits'. Habgood heeds history rather than feels it.

Heeding history is where Habgood finds common ground between symbol and function. Both the setting and the circumstance of his cathedra and his home helped. We are not concerned with the chronology of Habgood's years as Bishop of Durham nor with the events of that period. The way in which he sees and tackles problems, pursues opportunities and seeks reform are proper areas for consideration in this study.

The diocese of Durham is more manageable than many dioceses. In area it covers the county of Durham, together with that portion of Tyne and Wear that lies to the south of the Tyne and that portion of Cleveland that is north of the Tees. With a population of a little over one and a half million in an area of 1,015 square miles there are 262 parishes (237 benefices) with 315 churches served by just over 300 stipendiary clergy. There is a suffragan bishop (of Jarrow) and two archdeacons (Durham and Auckland).

It is easy to sketch plans for reforming the Church of England; for example, by multiplying bishops and dioceses. Supposedly, reform will bring the bishop nearer to his clergy so that he can father them! It would be little more than another form of paternalism. There is no ideal solution but there are pragamatic reasons for not wanting massive changes in the pattern of dioceses. Theological reasons for change are not conclusive and raise a further series of problems about provinces.

Habgood's manner of exercising episcope soon became clear and has not much changed. He entered his new work in post-synodical times but his style and his thinking are not strictly synodical. George Marchant, who served in the diocese from 1954 and was Archdeacon of Auckland from 1974 to 1983 gives a picture of perspective and contrast. He served during four episcopates.

> The first, Michael Ramsey (1952 to 1956) exercised a 'charismatic' episcopal style which meant that a number of leading clergy besides the archdeacons and the Diocesan

Board of Finance were administering 'bits' in their own way, but generally, the diocesan office with their help ran the diocese and the Diocesan Conference was very much a rubber stamp. Maurice Harland (1956 to 1966) brought in Mervyn Armstrong to be Bishop of Jarrow to try to get some grip upon problems then seen to be developing (for example, the need to deal with large and over-expensive vicarages), and himself set up supporting committees who roused suspicions and antagonisms by not being accountable to any elective structure in the diocese. They were 'faceless men'. Armstrong left just before Harland, and Ian Ramsey (1966 to 1973) – from his enthronement sermon onwards – had a vision of authority as what may be described as 'systemic', i.e. developing a common policy and gaining a shared 'mind' by openness to discussion; and Ian was nothing if not a great talker! Thus diocesan bodies – the Conference, Rural Deans' meetings and other *ad hoc* occasions were times for ventilating issues and preparing for the introduction of synodical government which fell to be done during that episcopate. Ian Ramsey had only two years after the actual introduction of synodical government.

Ramsey the warm-hearted talker was replaced by Habgood the cool appraiser and listener. There was much to appraise! The complexity of the diocesan organization with its multiplicity of sub-committees depressed Habgood. He was sure that the main purpose of central diocesan structures was to support, encourage and co-ordinate work done at the local level, and where necessary to relate this to the wider structures of society and the Church. Committees tend to serve and perpetuate themselves. After study and some experience Habgood put forward proposals for restructuring the diocese, proposals which were accepted by the Diocesan Synod in June 1974. The net effect of the organizational changes was to reduce the total number of committees, to cut out wasteful overlapping functions and to create better co-ordination between different aspects of diocesan activity.

George Marchant thinks that:

John Habgood tried to build up in the diocese through its structures both an awareness of corporate involvement and an increasingly informed and experienced participation in responsible self-government; while at the same time, he set perspectives and of course in matters of individual pastoral needs he acted on his own. Even there, most important matters would be discussed in staff meeting, or with even a slightly wider group. I may just mention that in all this structural reform, the Archdeacons, for the first time, were given a greater administrative role; perhaps it might be put that they were chosen to take that role. [Note: the other archdeacon, Michael Perry, was an Ian Ramsey not a Habgood appointment.]

Having said all this, it was a feature of John Habgood that he distanced himself from everyone. Living in Auckland Castle helped. But apart from the odd phone call (very infrequent) matters for discussion were preferably kept to staff meeting, or if necessary when one met him at a meeting, etc. It is possible that he was uneasy at having to make a judgement or decision – unless to ratify some fairly obvious course that simply needed a nod – when the occasion was requiring some other kind of attention, or gave little opportunity for proper examination. For he certainly encouraged the fullest examination of an issue and proper doing of 'homework' on matters for decision. Thus the wide and open participation involved a good deal more backroom work to prevent shoddy thinking and superficial policies. Of course, some unwise things could gain support, and needed to be quietly dropped or otherwise overruled; and similarly the 'structures' at times enabled the odd too strong-minded layman or cleric to get his head. The Bishop's Council was especially open to such, but on the whole it did well.

This raises the question – did all this make John Habgood remote as a figure? I suppose the answer is both yes and no. For while it surrounded his episcope with a dispersed network, so that most of the business of the diocese was done through others, yet it provided a number of occasions when, through representation, a not inconsiderable number of clergy and laity met him through his own presence at the Synods and Boards – quite apart from his constant presence in the parishes and deaneries. His

> manner was always cool; sometimes it seemed aloof, but at others, and always when personal need was involved, it could break into great kindness or almost youthful fun.

The persona and the style are one. Habgood appreciates that the Church has become organized in a bureaucratic style. Ideally the characteristics of bureaucratic organization are intended to make it possible to handle the complexities of modern societies without imposing intolerable strains on those who do so. There is division of responsibility, based usually on specialist knowledge. The complexity is chopped up into manageable bits. Unfortunately, as the organization grows so the circumference of the centre widens. In his presidential address to the Durham Diocesan Synod of November 1981 Habgood referred to the way in which people are moulded by bureaucracy. 'The values which sustain a bureaucratic system rub off on us, at least in terms of our public lives, and the more complex society becomes the more of life gets sucked into its orbit. In particular the impersonality of the system, an impersonality which is essential if it is to be fair, leads to the split between public and private life, between the efficient and the human, which lies at the root of so much frustration and such feelings of impotence and such blanket criticisms of the so-called "system".'

As Habgood sees it, there is no possibility that a complex body like a diocese or church could or should be run on a purely personal basis.

> This is what the pastoral system in the Church, existing alongside and as part of the synodical system, is supposed to represent. One of the arguments for bishops is that they provide a focus for personal action within the Church, in contrast with the impersonal activities of committees. There is truth in this. But any bishop, or anyone in a comparable position, who tried to take it literally, would quickly find the whole enterprise becoming unmanageable; and worse, he would quickly destroy the sense of fairness which is the main moral justification for bureaucracy.

In diocesan councils and in the committees of the General

Synod at Church House, Westminster, ways have to be found of

> redressing the balance between the efficiency of procedures, and the ultimate aim of declaring the love of God in Christ. It is a matter of style and sensitivity. It is the ability to present fairness and objectivity as themselves expressions of true pastoral concern, not just the dead hand of administrative convenience. It is the refusal to build little empires out of our separate spheres of responsibility; the willingness to cross the boundaries which our structures have all too often created. To fulfil a mission to bureaucratic structures is to discover how to handle power for the sake of those outside it (Sermon at service of Holy Communion for members of staff in Church House, Westminster, on 18 February 1986).

Despite being what is termed a good 'committee man', Habgood is not bureaucratically minded. His feeling is for independence and that includes his episcopate too. Alec Hamilton, a former Bishop Suffragan of Jarrow, who worked happily with Habgood, nonetheless recalls occasional difficulties.

> Difficulties, I believe, were largely caused by John's understanding of the role of a diocesan bishop. He was very conscious of the fact that the final authority rested in the hands of the diocesan bishop and that the diocesan bishop was in the driving seat. This meant that he tended to regard the suffragan bishop as a subordinate rather than a partner with whom the episcopal ministry in the diocese was shared, which was how I had been treated by both Maurice Harland and Ian Ramsey.
>
> After 1975 when nine suffragan bishops were elected to the General Synod the question arose as to whether or not the suffragans should be invited to attend Bishops' Meetings as well as meetings of the House of Bishops. The matter came up for debate in the House of Bishops and as the main spokesman for the suffragans I put their case. I was supported by the then Bishop of Kensington (Ronald Goodchild). After this John rose to speak and began by

> saying, 'I am afraid that I have got to disagree with my suffragan' and went on to say he was entirely opposed to suffragans attending Bishops' Meetings. He found himself in a minority of one, so did not get his way.

This incident throws light on Habgood's understanding of his episcopal ministry.

Habgood has a low view of suffragan bishops while retaining a high regard for the individuals who are suffragan bishops. He may feel that he cannot completely share his episcope with them but he delegates tasks and activities in trust and completeness. He allows those who serve him to take risks, and will back them up in risky areas if he feels their action has been thoughtfully and Christianly done. Michael Ball CGA, Habgood's own appointment as Bishop Suffragan of Jarrow in 1980, says with insight: 'If you don't believe in suffragans, I imagine you either give them an area where they act as diocesans or you merge them completely into your own ministry. The latter was the way John Habgood operated in this diocese.' Michael Ball quickly found that

> (Habgood's) character and mind are a unity, and in a way that quite a lot of people do not recognize. For instance, when he wrote his first letter to me asking if I would consider being his suffragan, the analysis of the pastoral situation in the diocese, and the needs for it, were a brilliant example of wonderful, clear pastoral thinking. Despite what people may imagine, he is able to think with his heart without it spoiling his head and able to think with his head without it spoiling his heart. He is also remarkably adept at being able to see where he himself is unable to function because of time and demands, and without envy or anything else, happy to leave such areas to other people. Everything is warmly calculated rather than coldly calculated.

'Calculation' is a word which is often used pejoratively. It need not be so used for it suggests realism. Habgood is nothing if not realistic. This extends to prayer about which he might be said to be 'calculating'. There are people in need, trouble and distress who need his prayers, and situations which demand them. His method is one of planned neglect. He prays for that person or a situation for, say, a fortnight, and then removes the name or cause from his list. Thereafter he leaves it to God.

Habgood, in exercising episcope – as symbol and function – is an example of Christian detachment. He enjoys his inheritance without being dependent on it. He receives it not by right but by grace.

Detachment is an ingredient in the episcopal life. It helps sound judgement and ensures mental stability and physical survival! Somehow a bishop has to be, however obscurely and inadequately, a visible representation to people of spiritual realities. Habgood says: 'To try to convey that spiritual reality, without losing touch with the world as it is, and without becoming submerged in the demands of a very large organization, is the special challenge and privilege of his job.'

While considering the episcopate, it is worth glancing at Habgood's presence at Lambeth Conferences, the ten-yearly gatherings of bishops from every diocese and province in the worldwide Anglican Communion.

At the 1988 Lambeth Conference there will be four sections: i Mission and Ministry; ii Dogmatic and Pastoral Concerns; iii Ecumenical Relations; and iv Christianity and Social Order. The choice of Chairman and Vice-Chairman for the fourth section is a scintillating contrast, for Habgood is Chairman and Desmond Tutu, Archbishop of Cape Town, is Vice-Chairman.

At the 1978 Lambeth Conference it was almost in reverse. Desmond Tutu (then General Secretary of the South African Council of Churches) was Chairman of section i, 'What is the Church for?' Habgood was Secretary of one of that section's eleven committees. The subject was twentieth-century technology and its relations to human life. The Chairman of the committee was Bruce Rosier, Bishop of Willochra, Australia and the other twelve bishops came from Canada, Mashonaland (now Zimbabwe), Mauritius, Ireland, Scotland, South America, North America, the Philippines and West Africa. The report of the committee is of minor note but interest focuses on two individuals in the group.

The strongest memory of Allen Goodings, Bishop of Quebec is of

> the interplay between two distinct types of persons. Both men had strong academic qualifications, both were committed to their vocation and both were seeking to determine the answer to the questions that had been passed to us. The major difference was in the style of each individual. Bishop Habgood was the typical reserved Briton; scientist, self-contained scholar and champion of orderly progression. John Spong [Bishop of Newark, USA] the liberal representative of the Episcopal Church, was a very impulsive outgoing person, almost to the state of being brash in his comments. Given the solid base from which either of them spoke, the variance in approach greatly enlivened our discussions and, I suspect, broadened the theories and insights offered and contributed greatly to the scope of our deliberations.

W. B. Spofford, then Bishop of Eastern Oregon, underlines the impression and thinks of Habgood as

> the 'in-house' specialist in nuclear technology and he was held in some 'awe' because, although most of us had strong feelings about the issues one way or another, in light of various traditions, biblical understandings etc., we also recognized that we were moving into highly technical fields. Throughout, I recall, Bishop Habgood, who was then of Durham, tended to be non-excitable; a reality-tester, a sharer of information and, in group dynamics terms, an 'enabler'. I, personally, found him to be a cogent thinker and leader of the group, without ever taking the role of chair away from Bruce Rosier . . . In our group, I recall, there tended to be 'conflict' between us Americans and the British on some of the issues, with the 'third world' constituency rather reflecting a 'your issues are not our issues' attitude. Reflection, by me at least, indicates that we were all right . . . and all wrong. Again, I do not recall Bp. Habgood being forceful in the group or, particularly, dominating the conversations or discussions, although he was, always, on 'top' of everything.

When John Spong of Newark first encountered Habgood at Lambeth he was convinced that he was

> England's number one stuffed shirt. He seemed to me to approach our study group from the vantage point of saying that he already had the answers and, if we would sit quietly at his feet, he would share his wisdom with us.
>
> I remember that my first impression of him did nothing except to motivate me to challenge him at every point and I did so with some regularity creating, I think, tension in that particular group. It was my feeling that as the days of the Lambeth Conference went by both of us came to a new awareness and definition of the other. I certainly came to respect his brilliance and his academic background and I had the feeling that he began to respect the fact that I, and others in the group, had contributions to make and comments that he had not yet even thought of.
>
> Before the time at Lambeth was over I considered my association with him to be among the most pleasant that the Lambeth Conference afforded me.

The Lambeth Conference of 1978 was one of the least memorable. With woefully inadequate preparation it was inevitable that resolution and conclusion would have a packaged effect. For section i there would have been little at all but for all-night sittings by Habgood and one of the consultants, David Jenkins (then Director of the William Temple Foundation, Manchester) putting pen to paper and giving necessary substance to the form of words!

11

The Widening Gap

Two unexpected aspects of Habgood's thought are his strong support for the established nature of the Church of England and his defence (or advocacy) of folk religion. The two are interconnected. How can they be justified?

In his recent book *Church and Nation in a Secular Age* Habgood defines folk religion in these terms:

> I intend to concentrate on those who see themselves as having some relationship, however tenuous, with the mainline Christian churches. These are the people who bring their children for baptism and want to be married and buried in church, and describe themselves on forms as C. of E., and who would be offended if they were described as un-Christian. Some of the outward signs of allegiance may be disappearing, but the evidence for a basic religiousness in human beings, even in a secular age, remains strong.

Is this really the case? The Church of England may be regarded as a kind of 'folk Church' of the English nation. It is certainly deeply embedded in the history and culture of the nation (the other word is buried!). At life's great moments – hatching, matching and despatching – it adds respectability and provides a magic charm, a kind of talisman to the simmering superstition of twentieth-century living. Is not this religion without responsibility encouraging works without faith? A wonderful illusion! The question is, does the Church of England care more about the preservation of illusion, and the maintenance of apathy for the sake of comfort, rather than for truth?

Then there is Establishment. The Church of England is the ancient Church of the land and by law established. Its chequered history needs no amplification here. There have been times of great power. There have been times when it was almost wholly subservient to the State. Indeed, the State played Jehovah and the Church was his Moses handing petitions up and tablets of the law down. The national Church has often stuck in the gullets of other Churches for it has been a Church to which every English man and woman by virtue of their nationality has a right to belong but no duty to obey. It is possible to participate in the privileges and flout the rules.

The twin pillar to Establishment is Endowment. Here is a Church feeding on the past. Long after virile life leaves it, the Church could continue to survive by this built-in transfusion service. But an imposing façade might conceal a ruin. There are some for whom the Establishment hangs about the Church as the dead albatross about the neck of the Ancient Mariner, troubling his conscience and embarrassing his movement. They want to find ways of removing the bird. Not so, Habgood!

Habgood accepts that most believers want a comfortable religion, something to take the strain out of living – and dying – and something to give a respectability to one's prejudices. Accepting that is no bad place to start for correction and conversion. The Church's role is that of servant, not of judge. Salt and light are its characteristics and they do their distinctive work by enhancing and illuminating what is already there – while themselves being transient.

Nevertheless, it is the force of the Church of England as a national Church, of its clergy directing their ministry towards a whole community rather than a limited membership role, which Habgood finds compelling. Again and again he uses the same argument, relying on the same analysis. In a letter to *Theology* (January 1977) he writes:

> For a variety of reasons, some good some bad, the Church of England still finds itself as the focus of identification for an inchoate mass of religious sentiment, which may only rarely come to the surface, but which may have great importance in people's lives nonetheless. My central contention is that, here and now at this point in history,

we hold this mass of sentiment in trust for the nation, and as a result we are constantly being given opportunities to turn it into something more recognizably Christian. Our present peculiar and difficult vocation as the Church of England is to acknowledge this historical inheritance and use it in the service of the Gospel. If we could widen the base of the establishment, and if we could find ways of representing both the cutting edge of the Gospel and the penumbra of varying degrees of faith which most actual churches seem to contain, we might be able to halt the otherwise apparently inevitable progression from the liberal to the secular State. At least I think it worth a try.

Habgood's theory was substantially reinforced and buttressed by experience as Bishop of Durham. In July 1973 he was at the traditional Miners' Service at Durham Cathedral. This is how he describes his experience: 'I have seldom felt more moved at the beginning of a service. There were the processions – very stiff, very solemn, very proud coming slowly, slowly towards me – which conveyed an overwhelming sense of the integrity of the occasion. These people were glad to be what they were. Their lives and their work were one.'

He soon discovered the reality of tightly-knit communities bound together by strands of joy and suffering, celebration and dismay, life and death. In short, solidarity. This was not soap-opera community. It was real. These men and their wives and families could still be proud even when the economic climate was bleak, getting still bleaker. Well away from the platitudes of the committee and conference chamber the big question for mining and other communities was, and is, How do you keep life significant in a world from which the cork has been pulled, a world from which much of the work that has filled it is dripping away?

When the miners demonstrated their unity in cathedral or church they were honouring and celebrating the past. It was Habgood's task to recognize that and find ways in which he could give them a sense of genuine hope for the future. At a miners' service in Blackpool (1977) Habgood knew he was preaching to men who were suffering or about to suffer. He showed how the gospel 'picks up the ordinary human experience of struggle and rivalry and disagreement and twists them round in the light of Christ's own dealing with human nature. And what it describes for us is a kind of wisdom, a kind of maturity which is worth celebrating: (1) The unity which grows out of compassion; (2) The gentleness rooted in strength; (3) The power to forgive and to bless which flows from God himself.'

Habgood is too intelligent to pretend that he identified or was able to identify with the miners. Visiting their clubs and 'downing' ale with them would have been patronizing humbug. Yet because he cares deeply for the bonds which hold people together as communities (and as a nation) he was able to speak to and for miners in ways and on occasions where he thought it would be effective. During the disastrous 1983/1984 miners' strike, Habgood grieved when already hard-pressed mining communities, under internal and external pressure, began to fall apart. Miner turned against miner. Thuggery and intimidation, arson and wanton destruction were no longer strangers to mining communities.

When the leader of Easington District Council, John Cummings, asked Habgood (by now Archbishop of York) to lend his support to a campaign to save pits in the Easington district, Habgood replied: 'I believe we owe it to future generations not to close pits before they are properly worked out, just as we owe it to the present generation not to destroy jobs until there is an overwhelming case for doing so . . . Knowing the district as I do, I am fully aware of the serious consequences which might follow the premature closing of pits. There is to my mind clear reason for caution about pit closures, in that they entail the irreversible abandonment of an energy source for the future' (April 1984).

The matter came into a heated question in the House of Commons when the Labour MP for Blyth Valley, John Ryman, asked the Prime Minister, Margaret Thatcher: 'Is the Prime Minister so conceited that she proposes to ignore the advice of even the bishops?' The Prime Minister, not unexpectedly, fielded the question with clear aim and succinctness: 'I do not propose to tangle with his Grace the Archbishop of York. But unless coal is as cheap and competitive as it could be, many jobs will be lost in other industries.'

Another Member of Parliament, Enoch Powell, did not mind tangling with Habgood and launched what Habgood referred to as, 'an extraordinary attack on my personal integrity'. *The Times* produced a headline which supported Powell's attack and suggested that Habgood supported the miners' strike. In a letter to *The Times* (2 May 1984) Habgood tried to set the record straight:

> It seemed to me at the time that the dispute was in danger of moving into areas about which rational discussion was impossible and my sole purpose in writing [to Cummings of Easington] was to remind my correspondents of the basis on which Durham's excellent record of negotiation might be continued. I did not see myself as either supporting the strike or condemning it. That is not my business. In fact when I wrote it I felt that my letter erred on the side of being platitudinous.
>
> Mr Powell based his attack on the sentence, 'I believe we owe it to future generations not to close pits before they are properly worked out'. By a very curious argument, which it is not necessary to repeat, he claimed that the word 'properly' could be interpreted as meaning, 'no longer capable of yielding coal that can be disposed of for not less than it costs to mine'.
>
> He then accused me of not admitting openly that this is what I meant and made this the basis of a charge of moral and religious bankruptcy. Mr Powell once had a reputation for clear and rigorous logic, but I must confess that the logic of this particular argument escapes me.
>
> The word 'properly', in the sentence which he subjected to such tortuous analysis, takes its colour from the previous paragraph about successful pit closures. The simple and only point I have been concerned to make is that there is a civilized way of dealing with pit closures in which all the human, economic and long-term effects are balanced against one another and used as a basis for negotiated agreements.
>
> It would be better for all concerned if those in the public eye tried to recapture this vision instead of indulging in foolish polemics.

Nonetheless the National Union of Mineworkers considered they had an ally at a time when they badly needed allies. At one stage in the dispute the Executive of the NUM asked the Church to help. The Church's view was that, if invited to listen and learn about the problems of the dispute, they would respond. The Archbishops of Canterbury and York (Runcie and Habgood) agreed that Habgood should lead a small ecumenical group to meet the NUM, which he did. By this time entrenchment was too deep and there were no practical results. Yet Habgood had much to offer. He refuses to think in terms of stereotypes – miners, workers or otherwise, pickets, police, trade unionists, government. There are real people behind the media-built up images. Habgood also takes care to keep close to reality which saves him and his words from being scooped up as media events, despite even Mr Powell's attempts to massage the words.

Habgood once wrote:

> In negotiating procedures it is often useful to move backwards and forwards between negotiating and analysing. When the bargaining process gets stuck, it is not a bad idea to pause deliberately, stop trying to bargain, and begin the process of shared analysis. If we can't agree on solutions, perhaps we can at least agree on what the problems are. And the more these are analysed by the contending parties side by side the more likely it is that some sort of common ground might be discovered. It seems to me that this concern for cool objective analysis is something which can apply equally well at the level on which most of us operate.

He could say this as one of his aims and ideals, yet in the knowledge that within its own life the Church of England's recent history is strewn with the corpses of failed attempts to unite, reconcile, and cohere on every major issue before it.

The mining dispute was an early warning system for a new industrial revolution. At the hub is unemployment. Habgood sees nothing but harm in the adversary politics of our time on this and other subjects. There have been and will be opportunities for him to say this and to put the reconciling view in the House of Lords. Preaching at an Industrial Service at St Paul's Cathedral (May 1981) Habgood expressed his unease at the growing division between the employed and the unemployed. 'Once people actually become unemployed they seem to drop out into a kind of no-man's land. They disappear from the various structures and interest groups and centres of power, which might otherwise give them a voice *within* the industrial system, rather than outside it. So the only voice left to them becomes the mass voice of marchers, and this alas can only make a noise without actually negotiating anything.'

Habgood is a person of hope. 'Hope inspires us to act, not just as individuals or trade unionists or consumers or economic units, but as human beings who have been judged, and given freedom by God to create our own future.' The prospect of the future looks different depending where one stands. Take one general view: that of computers, automation and similar technology. What do people see? Computer technology or automation creates an abundance of unemployment which some people cynically call leisure. (Computer technology also creates new jobs for a new élite.) Much mischievous talk takes place about leisure. A person who spends his day completing computer-oriented forms (he used to have to think about what he was doing) or pressing a button in an isolated corner of an automated factory (he used to turn a crank in a line with ten other men – he was not separate, tense or alone) in order to win his subsistence, is unlikely to feel disposed to spend his leisure in profitable self-education. In any case the 'right use of our leisure time' cannot be affixed from outside like an adhesive plaster, for it includes moral elements. As T. S. Eliot said, are we merely to be 'distracted from distraction by distraction'?

Christians have a duty to ask 'To what end is this change which is so affecting our lives?' Our age has been described as one of 'brilliance without wisdom, power without conscience'. Have we helped to make that a fact? It is a strange paradox that the material goals for which man has searched through the ages can, as we approach them, present such frightening and disturbing questions. We have assumed that work for most people consists of physical and/or mental effort. Is it possible for us to redefine our concept of work? Can we accept the prospect that people may engage in creative activity because of the drives of accomplishment or sheer pleasure rather than the necessity to work in order to eat? Can we devise a system of providing incomes to all as a matter of right, even though work in its traditional form will either no longer be performed or, if it is, be done in even smaller units of time? Can we discover the right use of, and an ethical basis for, computers in our society? The present task of all who care about humanity is to influence the shifting valuations of this age so that a better world may result from the transition. Are we content in an apathetically accepting kind of way to leave that special breed, 'other people', to wrestle with the problems and seek solutions to them? We must probe to the centre and not debate on the circumference of the problems. And we must be sensitive. If we fail to understand the opinions we oppose, we may fall into the effortless luxury of dismissing them as hypocrisy or propaganda; worse, we may fail to understand ourselves.

Perhaps most of all we must keep before us the ideal, namely the uniqueness of the individual, and fight against those who want to stick an increasing number of labels on us – en masse, of course! We must nourish those motives of kindness, tenderness and love which redeem men from hardness of heart, and which can make life tolerable, and sometimes noble, even when it becomes most tragic.

That is one general view. Now, look through Habgood's glasses. The whole competitive system on which traditional economies are based is a system of economic conflict. It is justified by a theory of evolution which attributes all development to the survival of the fittest. But are we so certain that conflict is a permanent good, or at least a built-in necessity? Habgood is sure that there is a stage at which co-operation can take the place of conflict without necessary loss of dynamism. After all, Christian teaching about marriage and the family has assumed that here at least is one social unit which does not and should not depend upon conflict for vitality.

Habgood rebukes those who rant about inevitability. He asks, for example,

> Why must we assume that technology can only be used to replace human skills, rather than enhance them? That it

> cannot encourage better craftsmanship rather than destroy it? And if it is claimed that we are driven towards devaluing skills by economic necessity, then again I ask what kind of necessity is this? And isn't it true that in the past economics has often given an air of necessity to indefensible practices which weren't in fact necessary at all? Determinism is a cheat. It denies the God-given possibilities of change.

Habgood has examined many panaceas and approved some of them, such as job-sharing. Selfishness gets in the way of realizing most of them. The trouble is that most of the suggested remedies would do little more than touch the fringes of the problem. As a fact-facer Habgood knows that as human beings we can now produce far more than we can ever consume, and it seems to him to follow inevitably that many people will not actually be required to produce anything, or even to service the production of anything. 'So what do we do?' he asked in an address on 'Work, unemployment and the Church' for the St Catherine's Mill (CATS) project in Leeds (14 May 1984):

> Part of what we can do is to rethink the rules of the game; to demonstrate in practical ways that human worth does not have to be linked to weekly wages. We can begin a process of decoupling – between wages and human worth – and that is where the Churches have a unique opportunity to lead the way. It is central to the Christian gospel that we human beings are not justified in God's eyes by what we do. We are loved by him for what we are. And in that distinction lies a fundamentally important affirmation about what it is that gives us our human dignity and value. In the end, it is not the size of our pay packet, or the importance of our job, which matters most. It is our acceptance of ourselves as worthwhile people. Thus, the most essential thing is for people to have a setting and the kind of encouragement to go with it, through which they can discover their own worthwhileness. And if this happens, then they are set free to do things for themselves and for each other and for the whole community; whether they are paid for it or not.
>
> It is this kind of setting which CATS aims to provide.

It is a place where the unemployed can discover that even if they can't be employed for wages, they nevertheless have talents and skills and interests which can be employed for the enrichment of the life of the whole community. Encouragement of the arts is one obvious way to release such talents, but there are others which no doubt will come to seem equally important as the project develops.

These big questions of our time are being considered in a project called 'Goals for our future society' launched by the Church of England Board for Social Responsibility. Responses from the Church and from society were invited after the issuing of a consultative document. Replies and comments have been considered by a working party chaired by Habgood, and a report is to appear in 1987. Habgood's own views on the subject have been influenced by the writings of that weighty and widely respected modern theologian, Karl Rahner. Like Rahner, Habgood advocates 'morality without moralizing'. Rahner has pointed to the need for 'a very important change of emphasis in Christian proclamation: consciences must be formed, not primarily by the way of casuistical instruction, going into more and more concrete details, but by being roused and trained for autonomous and responsible decisions in the concrete, complex situations of human life which are no longer completely soluble down to the last detail, in fields never considered by the older morality, precisely because they were then unknown and even now cannot be adequately mastered by a rational casuistry.' In other words, as Mahoney has written, 'The role for the Churches is not intensified moral instruction which provides pre-packaged answers, but sustained moral education.'

Habgood considers that the Church of England can still play a vital part in 'sustained moral education'. It will do so only if it can itself unite across dogmas and divisions around the person of Jesus. Then it can use its special gifts, qualities and insights to meet the issues of the day. Among these special gifts, qualities and insights are, in Habgood's words, 'breadth of vision, the ability to handle complexity and to live with polarities, moral concern rooted in basic principles rather than detailed prescriptions, wide pastoral contacts and commitments, a recognized place both in the voluntary sector and as an integral part of national life, a sense of responsibility for the whole nation constantly tempered by broader international and religious perspectives, a realistic appraisal of our human capacity to deceive ourselves and serve our own interests, a message of hope in the face of failure, cynicism and despair'.

Moving these phrases from platitude to practice is not easy. It may be not what the nation wants from the Church but it is probably what it needs. The recited qualities are not ones that will earn instant applause or a ready hearing. Changing the atmosphere for 'sustained moral education' is a Sisyphean task. Habgood will continue pushing the stone up the hill.

It is not only on national issues that Habgood is working. His involvement with the Church and Society sub-unit of the World Council of Churches is global. Habgood heads a committee whose purpose is to promote interdisciplinary reflection and action by theologians, scientists and others concerned with the common responsibility of individuals and churches in modern society. Its work is divided into four core groups: theology of nature (of which Habgood is a member); the value of life and life-centred ethics; ecumenical social ethics; and society, technology and environment: church responses. The seventeen participants, led by Habgood, come from all parts of the world. There will be case studies: for example, deforestation in Central America; appropriate technology in East Africa; education on nuclear issues in the Pacific; church responses to unemployment in Western Europe.

The sub-unit has a dual task. Its members should be able to respond to urgent topical issues which fall within their mandate, as the issues arise, such as the Bhopal and Chernobyl disasters. In doing so, they have to resist becoming moral busybodies with an appropriate response to every fleeting issue, however important these problems may appear to be at the time. Speaking to the spirit of the age with cogency and clarity is more difficult than speaking against the spirit of the age, although that is necessary too on many issues. If the Church and Society sub-unit or any other of the WCC's committees is going to have anything worthwhile to say, it must have a theological base and sound technical credentials. That is the other part of its dual task. In Habgood's group it is accepted that 'the Churches lack a credible theology of nature which takes into consideration the discoveries and insights of biblical studies, science and dialogue with other religious traditions and ideologies. Such a theology has to take into account the rich tradition of the Orthodox Churches in their holistic approach towards the created order. It should include the relation of God to the origin and evolution of life as seen by science. In addition, the study group will attempt to analyse the different views of nature, especially the dominant view developed in the seventeenth century and reinforced by the Enlightenment'.

I began this chapter by looking at folk religion. One aspect of folk religion is language. Deeply embedded in the psyche of English people is the language of the Book of Common Prayer. Its words can have a haunting quality of poetic stirring, expressing the inexpressible, even among the irreligious. It is ironic that the stalwart of folk religion is regarded as the toppler of the Book of Common Prayer. It is untrue, but myths have a habit of sticking. In January 1974 the Archbishop of Canterbury (Michael Ramsey) on behalf of himself and the Archbishop of York (Donald Coggan) invited Habgood to take on the chairmanship of a General Synod working party to consider the proposal for a People's Service Book (note the words). Habgood accepted, 'although I cannot pretend to be enormously enthusiastic at the prospect' (letter to Archbishop of Canterbury, 2 February 1974). The story of Habgood as a liturgical reviser is a book in itself. Here we are concerned with only one aspect of it. Habgood carried responsibility, since its inception, for the Alternative Service Book, which was intended to be a major supplement to the Book of Common Prayer. In practice it has widely replaced it. More than anything else Habgood's work with the ASB brought him to the forefront of the General Synod and onto a national platform. There were no prizes, only rotten eggs to be thrown at a man who was accused of many things including killing the Lord's Prayer. Instead of being heard and heeded as an authoritative voice on ethical issues Habgood ran the gauntlet of abuse on a subject not of his own choosing. Little wonder that the General Synod did not embrace him with any enthusiasm. His own lack of enthusiasm for the General Synod is conveyed, albeit unintentionally, in an article 'On being a liturgical reviser' (*Theology*, March 1979):

> The synodical system itself, which is basically a system of decision-making by committees, militates against creative innovation. A draft service, as it leaves the Liturgical Commission, is the product of many hours of committee work. It then has to run the gauntlet of at least one scrutiny by the House of Bishops, two full Synodical debates, and a Revision Committee stage during which any member of the General Synod can suggest and, by personal attendance at the Committee, press for detailed amendments. Dissatisfied members can further press their amendments during the second General Synod debate provided they can find a certain minimum backing. All this is done in a context where differing churchmanships and other interests are carefully balanced against each other, and it is hardly surprising, therefore, if the results have an air of compromise about them. A frequent question has to be – 'Will the Synod accept this?' and those who have the task of piloting material through the Synod know full well that there are limits. This is a basic fact about liturgical revision, and though the Church of England may have tied itself up more tightly in procedural knots than any other Church, no doubt the same constraints operate in lesser degrees elsewhere.
>
> The other side of this synodical coin is the fact that the Synod is composed of people who, by and large, are interested in church government, and who thus are likely to have a greater concern for reform, even very modest reform, than the average churchgoer. A body like the Synod is not, and never can be, fully representative, and can easily get out of touch both with the large constituency of conventional infrequent church attenders who want things to remain as they used to be, and with the unknown constituency of unconventional half-believers who long for the Church to modernize itself. The pace of liturgical revision

which it encourages, therefore, is likely to be criticized as too fast by some and too slow by others.

When the Alternative Service Book was finally published in November 1980, it was met with a cascade of criticism. There were petitions in plenty and the Prayer Book Society (founded in 1975) mobilized opposition. The widespread dissatisfaction with the Book of Common Prayer from the beginning of the century onwards, and the extent to which unauthorized alternatives were in common use, had been conveniently forgotten. One of Habgood's hopes for the ASB was that it would stabilize and regularize the worship of the Church of England for ten years or more, thus giving the Church time to assess the changes and discover how well the new liturgies wear in practice. It would also mean that people would be encouraged to own a prayer book again rather than the multiplicity of booklets which had been made available.

The shrillest attacks came from the arts and universities but also from other distinguished and respected people in public life. The press bias against the ASB was almost unanimously adverse. The choice of reviewers ensured that: for example, Marghanita Laski in *The Times* (20 November 1980) and Beryl Bainbridge in the *Sunday Telegraph* (9 November 1980). Habgood had answered many private letters received during the period of his work with the ASB. Now he was penning letters to the press. He made mincemeat out of some reviews which were most noticeable for their malice and lack of objectivity. Inaccuracies and innuendoes were pinpointed and pricked. Whatever Habgood said about the virtues of the Book of Common Prayer and his emphasis on the word 'Alternative' in ASB (a point which is made in the Preface he wrote to the ASB), he was seen as a strenuous advocate of the new book.

During 1979, when the petitioning season was in full literary flood, Habgood replied to some signatories in a letter to *The Times* (20 November 1979). After stressing that the ASB would be an addition to, not a replacement for, the Prayer Book, he makes some interesting points.

> Our culture has been passing through a long period of radical change, change to which many of the signatories of

> the original petition have themselves contributed. Now, with so many of the familiar landmarks gone, they seize on one, the continuity of language, and ask the Church to preserve it by insulating itself against the processes of cultural erosion.
>
> I accept that this may indeed be part of the Church's task, a part of special importance to many who exist only on the fringes of church life. To others, though, the continuity sought for and expressed is primarily a continuity of symbol and action, and in preserving this the newer forms may be often more effective than the old. For such people, the new-found ability to distinguish the Eucharist, say, from the particular words in which it is celebrated, has come as a spiritual enrichment, and there is understandable resistance to any excessive claims for one kind of language.

Habgood may think that the ASB is a proper development in the Church's progress but he is not swept overboard by its language. However, there is more than language. Writing on the 'Pros and cons of liturgical revision' in *The Times Higher Education Supplement* (14 December 1979) he noted:

> My guess is that, given one of the consequences of liturgical revision as a shift in emphasis towards symbols and actions and away from the precise words which interpret them, we might expect a greater mutual acceptance of different traditions, at least within church circles, and hence, paradoxically, a partial antidote to fragmentation within the very process of change.
>
> The point is at least worth debating. So too is the wider question whether it is reasonable for academics to expect the Churches to bear this cultural burden (i.e. cultural continuity) alone when they have themselves done much to drive the Churches into isolation.

An aside from Habgood was also included in this article, namely, 'a personal dislike for junketings around during the giving of the Peace in the Eucharist. There are times when a brief mutual acknowledgement of one another can be entirely appropriate and very moving. If ever the Churches succeed in covenanting together, the giving of the Peace will be a highly significant action. But a Sunday by Sunday handshake all round can be both artificial and embarrassing and can hide the vertical dimension, the crucial acknowledgement that each of us needs to receive God's peace if we are to communicate together.'

Habgood himself is deeply and prayerfully helped by poetry. Poetry enlarges his imagination and sensibilities. His bookshelves disclose the importance of poetry to him: well-thumbed pages and, as with all his bookshelves, new volumes as well as old. 'The limits of my language are the limits of my world' is a salutary saying. Habgood's world is for exploration and poetry is food for the journey.

For all Habgood's advocacy of folk religion he nonetheless realizes that so far as the Church of England is a national Church, it operates in an increasingly secular and pluralistic society. This is the major theme of his book *Church and Nation in a Secular Age* (1983). The gap is widening, but Habgood does not want to unchurch anyone. He argues that, 'if the Church were to decide that it was over-burdened by establishment, or if it were to go searching for some imagined new freedom, or if it were to restrict itself deliberately to a small group of activists then . . . disestablishment would be both a symptom of and a recipe for decline.'

The book was researched and written during a six-month sabbatical after Habgood had been at Durham for ten years. During these ten years there had been many changes 'at the top' in the Church. Frederick Donald Coggan as Archbishop of York, who had consecrated Habgood, moved to Canterbury in 1975. A recognized caretaker Primate (a phrase he turned to his advantage), Coggan retired in 1980. He was succeeded by Robert Alexander Kennedy Runcie.

Meanwhile, at York, Coggan had been succeeded by Stuart Yarmouth Blanch (previously Bishop of Liverpool) and he announced his retirement in February 1983.

Although speculation was rife following Blanch's retirement, it was inevitable and proper that Habgood should move to York. When controversial Edward Norman, Dean of Peterhouse College, Cambridge wrote in the *Sunday Telegraph* (20 February 1983) on the qualities needed in a new Archbishop of York, he stated: 'What the Church needs is a balance of talents at the top: pastors, scholars, administrators, and even saints. Habgood qualifies under more than one of those categories.'

12

Living with Paradox

John Stapylton Habgood was enthroned as the ninety-fifth Archbishop of York in York Minster on 18 November 1983. He is the first whose enthronement was attended by a Prime Minister (Margaret Thatcher).

In his sermon Habgood emphasized the importance of public faith of which the enthronement was a spectacular expression. But if public faith is to be effective it must be found, assembled and contained in a framework. Habgood said: 'What is lacking is a focused awareness, a public frame, a shared faith, which can sharpen vague feelings into prayer and commitment and action. But how is it possible to begin to refocus in a society so fragmented, so critical, so suspicious of authority? And how dare an archbishop, how dare a ceremony like this, witness to the need for a public framework of faith without seeming impertinent or blind?

'Here lies a lifetime's work. But it is a work which I am convinced, under God, is possible and I want to offer just one hint about where to start. I see no ultimate contradiction between relying on a coherent public framework of faith and being critically aware of its limitations. In fact it is only by alternating between belief and doubt that we come to know anything at all.'

Habgood's message for the Church was a disturbing one for those who had ears to hear. There would be radical criticism. 'That is why a public faith can never be a settled static order. That is why the Church must be for ever building and for ever pulling down; for ever thankful for what it has received and for ever conscious of its inability to receive it in all its fullness. It is in the combination of these two, in the match between the believing heart and the critical mind, that true faith grows strong.'

Under Habgood's leadership the Church will have to deepen its faith and sharpen its intellect, if it is to respond to his challenge.

Faith and intellect are also the concerns of David Jenkins, Bishop of Durham. On 14 March 1984 it was announced that fifty-nine-year-old David Jenkins, Professor of Theology at Leeds University, was to be Habgood's successor as Bishop of Durham, although Jenkins sees himself as more the successor to Ian Ramsey than to Habgood. The appointment was unexpected and interesting. Jenkins had not been involved with the institutional life of the Church of England, although he was very well known through his membership of committees and working parties. He was also well known as a lecturer, as a performer who thinks, and thinks theologically, on his feet with sparkling, scintillating and sometimes stinging words flowing in endless torrents. The words are not necessarily there to be analysed. He had been used to freedom as chaplain of an Oxford college, while on the staff of the World Council of Churches, as Director of the William Temple Foundation and as a university professor. As a bishop there were to be some boundaries to his activities but no limits to his tongue. Habgood knew Jenkins to be a man with a great ability to stimulate belief and build up believers and he was familiar with Jenkins's books. Habgood, in personal terms, would not agree with the way in which Jenkins makes some of his statements.

This is not the place to labour the apocalyptic times through which the Church of England has been passing, but mention of Habgood's crucial part in the furore leading to Jenkins's consecration cannot be avoided. It was not long before Jenkins was involved in serious controversy, most particularly by his remarks made on television and in interviews, notably in the television programme 'Credo' on 29 April 1984 and again on 24 June 1984. In the 29 April programme Jenkins, who was being interviewed by Philip Whitehead, was asked whether the story of the Virgin Birth was historically and literally true. He replied: 'The Virgin Birth I'm pretty sure is a story told after the event in order to express and symbolize a faith that this Jesus was a unique event from God . . . I wouldn't put it past God to arrange a Virgin Birth if he wanted, but I very much doubt if he would, because it seems contrary to the way in which he deals with persons and brings his wonders out of natural personal relationships.'

These and other remarks were seized upon by many people as evidence of a heretical bishop-elect. A nationwide petition addressed to Habgood and organized by the Revd W. D. Ledwich of Hereford (who has since left the Church of England) alleged that Jenkins denied 'the Virgin Birth and the Resurrection of our Lord to be historical events and also that belief in Jesus as God-made-flesh is necessary for a Christian'. The petitioners asked Habgood to invite Jenkins to affirm publicly that he believed the Creeds as the Church had consistently interpreted them; and that, should he refuse, Habgood should seriously question whether it was right to proceed with the consecration. This placed Habgood at the centre of the clamour. If anyone could stop Jenkins from becoming a bishop, it was Habgood. They didn't know Habgood! Twelve thousand people signed the petition which was presented to Habgood on 1 July 1984.

Some clergy in the diocese of Durham had been much disturbed by Jenkins's views and some proctors of the Convocation of York asked Habgood to defer the consecration. The Church of England was in uproar and the non-church-going and non-believing public were beginning to take note. Meanwhile, on 22 May, Jenkins issued some notes in which he tried to direct people away from 'Credo' to his books *The Glory of Man* and *The Contradiction of Christianity*. He stated that 'the original "Credo" programme was built around my explaining how and why I personally believe and make the traditional Christian claim that Jesus was both truly God and truly man'. But Jenkins had become a media man and it was somewhat odd, even disingenuous, to say 'it might make a very valuable contribution to rebuilding communication, trust and community in our divided society if Christians always exercised great restraint in responding to all media events and relied on patient inquiry before they reacted to them.'

Habgood touched on this in his measured response to questions of principle in the Ledwich petition:

> The first concerns the role of the mass media, and whether a bishop's orthodoxy should be judged by his writings, the general tenor of his teaching and his formal profession of faith, or by brief, unscripted and epigrammatic remarks made to the media. How important, in other words, is his media image, especially when it differs markedly from what he knows himself to be?
>
> It can be argued that Professor Jenkins has been unwise in the manner he has expressed himself publicly. No doubt he will quickly learn that the way a bishop is heard differs from the way a professor is heard, and that the impression conveyed through the media may be more significant than what is actually said or left unsaid. In any attempt to communicate profound truths, public relations cannot be ignored. Nevertheless, it would be a strange reflection on the Church's integrity if in so important a matter as the choice of a man to be bishop, it were to pay more attention to the image than to the reality (letter from Habgood to Ledwich, 1 July 1984).

Jenkins had some interesting reflective thoughts on the matter when he wrote in *The University of Leeds Review* (1984/5, vol. 27) on 'Professors, bishops and the search for truth'.

> The disturbing personal experience of the trivializing of truth by the media is matched by equally disturbing evidence of an absence of a concern for truth among the self-styled defenders of Christian faith and orthodoxy. Among the articles known to me and in the letters received by me there was hardly any discussion of the case for holding that what I said was *true*. The discussion almost wholly centred round whether I, as a bishop-designate, should say such things. I even received letters from quite respectable and senior clergymen, which suggested that a professor of theology (who was a believing Christian) was quite entitled to pursue such questions in such a way, but a bishop was not. I felt obliged to reply to at least two such writers that their suggestions seemed to me to be, from the point of view of Christian faith in God, precious close to blasphemy and, from the point of view of simple human logic, identical with nonsense. On the one hand the pursuit

> of truth was to be suppressed or ignored in the interests of a responsibility to God and his Church, on the other a mere shift of institutional responsibility apparently justified two different and incompatible sets of truth values and criteria for truth.

Again, Habgood had pursued this topic in his reply to Ledwich, when he wrote:

> Is there a special obligation on a bishop as teacher and defender of the faith, to have a different standard of truth from that of other Christians? The question is not whether his faith is greater and more mature; it is to be hoped that it is. But in so far as certain historical events are affirmed to be true a bishop, like everyone else, must depend upon the historical evidence. His role as teacher, therefore, is not independent of the intellectual and spiritual task of the whole Church, as in each generation it seeks to answer questions about truth for itself. Within this total task of the Church bishops and academic theologians have different roles, and often ask different questions, but it would surely be wrong to imply that as teachers they should have different standards.
>
> A bishop's role as a defender of the faith is part of his corporate responsibility as a member of the whole episcopate, and is expressed synodically through some of the special powers conferred on the House of Bishops. Changes in the official teaching of the Church on doctrinal matters involve elaborate procedures and widespread consultation, and cannot be inferred, as the petition suggests, from the interplay between differing episcopal views which is one of the factors maintaining the comprehensive character of our Church.

Near the nub of the petitioners' case was that the Church of England requires its clergy to profess belief in the Catholic Creeds. Yes – and in a particular interpretation of them. For Habgood the position was not that clear and easy and could not be for any Church 'which takes seriously both the continuity of its faith and the processes of historical change'. He relied on the 1938 Report on Doctrine which 'recognized that the Creeds contain many types of statement in which the borderline between the symbolic and the historical dimensions cannot be precisely defined', and it explicitly affirmed a liberty of interpretation. It was careful, however, to stress that such liberty must not be taken so far as to undermine the historical basis of the gospel itself. In its own words: 'It is essential to hold that the facts underlying the gospel story – which story the Creeds summarize and interpret – were such as to justify the gospel itself.' To this extent the 1938 Report provides backing for the statement in the notes to the Ledwich petition that 'we are not at liberty to reinterpret the Scriptures and Creeds in a way which denies their content'. But unlike the petition, the report did not conclude from this affirmation of the historical basis of Christianity, that everything stated in a historical form must necessarily be interpreted as literal history.

Another controversy surrounded the 'Credo' poll on bishops' beliefs. Two researchers telephoned diocesan bishops, and baited and hooked thirty-one of them. During the conversation four 'questions' were asked. Did the bishop feel the Virgin Birth was 'historically' true or a later addition to emphasize divinity? Were the miracles (mentioning in particular the walking on the water and the changing of water into wine) literal or illustrative of divinity? Was the resurrection a physical return (flesh and blood) or an 'experience'? How is a Christian defined? The results of the so-called 'poll' were splattered across the television screens and the newspapers but the results needed treating with great caution. It was not a properly conducted 'poll'. The bishops did not know they were being 'polled'. The methodology was almost non-existent. It was conversation rather than direct question and answer. The researchers summed up, perhaps even decided, what the bishops believed. It was highly subjective, with no checks and balances. Habgood wrote harshly of what he called 'this extraordinary exercise'. 'I suppose it is one of the vices of our television age that we like to slot people into nice little categories which totally ignore the complexities of real life, count them, and then imagine we have achieved something significant. The crudities of this particular poll were a bit like asking people what they think of freezers, aeroplanes, nuclear energy and the Horse of the Year Show, and then classifying them as being for or against "the modern world" ' (York Diocesan Leaflet, September 1984).

On the question of postponing the consecration of Jenkins there was never any doubt. Jenkins had issued a written statement: 'I shall unhesitatingly respond affirmatively before God, in complete good faith and in total dependence on his grace, to the question which the Archbishop puts to a Bishop-elect at his consecration, "Will you affirm your loyalty to this inheritance of faith as your inspiration and guidance under God in bringing the grace and truth of Christ to this generation and making him known to those in your care?" '. 'The inheritance of faith' includes the Scriptures, the catholic Creeds and the historic formularies of the Church of England.

Habgood accepted this statement and challenged Jenkins's opponents to back their charges by evidence from his writings and other well-considered expressions of belief.

As Archbishop a great deal of Habgood's time was taken up in dealing with 'the Jenkins affair'. It was a very distracting period for him when many other issues were pressing on his time and attention. Yet it provoked him to write an interesting and widely appreciated letter on 'Christian believing' in the York Diocesan Leaflet (July 1984). He made the point that all theologians fail in their task, for they are limited to human language whereas 'all true theology culminates in the prayer of silent adoration'.

He referred to the Creeds as 'permanent signposts of Christian orthodoxy. But in interpreting them the same principle applies as in interpreting the Scriptures on which they are based. Each generation of Christians has to use the best scholarship available to get back into the minds of those who first experienced the impact of Christ's coming, and endeavoured to put it into words . . . The essential thing, and the true test of orthodoxy, is not whether we would use this or that precise form of words if we were writing the Creeds today, but whether through them we can discern the authentic vision and experience to which they bear witness.'

After considering the doctrine of the Virgin Birth, Habgood summarized his thinking in this way:

> As Christians we believe that God has done a new thing in Jesus Christ, revealing himself in a human life, subject to the ordinary conditions of humanity. The historical reality of this new thing is attested by the New Testament and by 2,000 years of Christian experience.
>
> The doctrine of the Virgin Birth is a powerful symbol of this truth, but it is not the only means by which the truth can be expressed or safeguarded.
>
> Evaluation of the doctrine has to rely more on judgements about its theological appropriateness than on historical study.

Some of Habgood's fellow bishops, notably Hugh Montefiore, Bishop of Birmingham, thought Habgood should have dealt with Jenkins in a similar way to that in which Randall Davidson, Archbishop of Canterbury, dealt with Herbert Hensley Henson. Davidson persuaded Henson to agree to a statement before consecration and there was an exchange of letters. Instead Habgood went ahead with the consecration on 6 July 1984 (the Feast of St Thomas More). There were more protests, culminating in a General Synod debate, and the request to the House of Bishops to reflect on the debate, the result of which was the 1986 report of the House of Bishops: *The Nature of Christian Belief*.

Two days after Jenkins's consecration Habgood was preaching to members of the General Synod in York Minster (8 July 1984), urging them not to be surprised or shocked by conflict. 'Don't be content with it either. See it as an invitation to look deeper, to think and act more charitably, and to catch the light from another facet of the diamond of God's glory.'

'If conflicts have to be faced and if some conflicts at least are endemic, what holds us together? What can help us to tolerate conflict and work our way through it?'

The answer is worship.

> Worship can heal us because the more it penetrates below the surface of mere words, the more the different streams of interpretation can converge on their source. Dare we say that those who worship and love Christ in their hearts in the light of their different traditions are really worshipping *different* Christs? Or can we say that here, in the mystery

> of adoration, adoration of the *one* Christ, the conflicts which otherwise loom so large are just the raw material of growth?

The day after this sermon York Minster was struck by lightning, with disastrous results. That too is another story.

Although Habgood is for national unity and cohesiveness, he also has a feeling for the Northern Province as a unity. This is no bad thing, and it may do something to counteract the baleful influence of London bureaucracy and what appears to be increasing centralization despite protests to the contrary.

Habgood is visiting each of the northern dioceses and spending several days in each. Colin James came north from being Bishop Suffragan of Basingstoke to be Bishop of Wakefield. He has returned whence he came, to be Bishop of Winchester. He has an interesting reflection. Writing before he left for Winchester he noted:

> I felt a much stronger sense of cohesion in Church life, and in Episcopal ministry, in the Northern Province than I ever did in the South. The Yorkshire Bishops, i.e. Bradford, Ripon, Sheffield and Wakefield meet regularly, together with the Bishop of Southwell. And we have also had fairly frequent meetings with the same Yorkshire Group and our opposite numbers in the Roman Catholic and Free Churches. This has had a further dimension with the annual Conferences at Scargill for all Church Leaders in the North. They have been going for a good many years now since the time that Archbishop Coggan launched The Call to the North. Another domestic factor is that when we have Consecrations of Bishops at York Minster most of us are able to attend and this is followed by a lunch at St William's College with our wives present, and this too reinforces a sense of fellowship. Since Archbishop Habgood came we have had one or two meetings of the Northern Bishops on our own.

Perhaps the sturdy independence of the Northern Province will be more evident in a corporate way. It already shows in individuals in dioceses as varied and diverse as York, Durham, Blackburn, Bradford, Carlisle, Chester, Liverpool,

Manchester, Newcastle, Ripon, Sheffield, Sodor and Man, Southwell and Wakefield.

Naturally, Habgood, as Archbishop of York, is involved with the major issues on the Church's agenda. He has disappointed the supporters of the Movement for the Ordination of Women. They had hoped to draw him into the open, which means that they looked for active support for their cause (or battle, as it has become). It does not appear that they will take 'No' for an answer which is very unhealthy in a Christian Church with a synodical form of government. Habgood's position is clear: 'I am myself in favour of the ordination of women, while at the same time trying hard to understand and be sympathetic towards those who oppose it. I am very conscious of how deeply divisive the issue is, both ecumenically and within the Anglican Communion, and this is why I believe change, if and when it comes, will have to come slowly.' It is not an issue which is high on his list of priorities.

Habgood regards it as much more important to look at what is happening in society and to give a view. He is concerned about how individualistic, in a bad sense, people are becoming. 'The danger of an enterprising society is that each one looks after himself.' He has for example been active in opposing the Shops Bill with its clause abolishing the Sunday Trading Regulations. His opposition sprang 'from a gut feeling that something precious is in danger of being destroyed'. Writing to his diocese (March 1986) Habgood said: 'The days of the week, the special character of the weekend, the day that is visibly different, these are landmarks in any otherwise undifferentiated progression of time. It is part of our human genius, not only to divide up our experience into manageable blocks of time but also to give them different flavours, different atmospheres, different textures.'

> There is evidence that the observance of one day in seven as a day of rest is even older than the Old Testament. References to the Sabbath in the first chapter of Genesis and in the Ten Commandments look very like the reaffirmation of a social landmark which already existed. This particular way of structuring human life, therefore, at least in Jewish, Christian and Muslim civilizations, belongs to

> the very roots of our social organization. The fuss about Sunday springs from the feeling that these roots are threatened . . . In itself Sunday trading is a small thing . . . But the protection of our social landmarks is a big thing. And those whose actions might threaten them have to be reminded by all possible means that immediate political advantage or administrative convenience are not appropriate criteria when fundamental issues are at stake.

It is time to take our leave of Habgood, an idealist without illusions. He may not yet be at the height of his powers or at the peak of his influence. A study of the words and works of a living man does not end with conclusions. The work is funnel-shaped. Moving towards the rim we can look at two final pictures.

Habgood is well aware of his vulnerability. He has no false illusions about himself or the office he holds. Any holder of public office today is in danger of fantasy, for the expectations are unreal to the point of absurdity. Preaching at the Beverley Festival Service for civic leaders (29 April 1984) he asked:

> How do we protect ourselves from fantasy? By self-knowledge? By an inner integrity? By awareness of our limitations? By a deep inner strength and purpose? By all these things. But perhaps the best place to begin is with the simple vision: by looking at Jesus, this Jesus whom we crucified, and whom God has made both Lord and Christ.
>
> Alas for those who have no simple vision. Let me quote from one of the wisest spiritual writers of our day, the monk Thomas Merton. 'He who attempts to act or do things for others or for the world without deepening his own self-understanding, freedom, integrity and capacity to love, will not have anything to give others. He will communicate to others nothing but the contagion of his own obsessions, his aggressiveness, his ego-centred ambitions, his delusions about ends and means, his doctrinaire prejudices and ideas. There is nothing more tragic in the modern world than the misuse of power to which men are driven by their misunderstanding of themselves.'

The Northern Province has at its head a man who has a

simple vision at the heart of the complexities and burdens surrounding him.

We can recall his enthronement, when he said: 'I can't escape a verse from Psalm 11, itself written in an age of uncertainty and division: "If the foundations are destroyed, what can the just man do?" '

'Public faith is about the foundations; it is about the things which bind us together, and the values we share, and the goals we pursue. The psalmist refuses to separate this concern with foundations from individual personal goodness and faith. "What can the just man do?" '

Habgood has said: 'My Christian faith allows me, indeed encourages me, to hold on to opposites; and this enlarging function is part of the meaning it has for me.'

It also helps him to live with paradox.

Bibliography

This selective bibliography does not include Habgood's many book reviews and short articles, nor his contributions to parish magazines at Kensington and Jedburgh, or to *Regina*, the magazine of Queen's College, Birmingham. Neither does it include his monthly letters to the diocese of Durham ('The Bishop's Letter') which really were letters, occupying the whole leaflet. They covered contemporary issues facing Church, nation and society. His letters in the York Diocesan Leaflet are less frequent but again tackle one subject in as much detail as space allows.

BOOKS

Religion and Science, Series on Science and Society, Mills & Boon 1964. Republished by Hodder & Stoughton 1972

A Working Faith, Essays and Addresses on Science, Medicine and Ethics, Darton Longman & Todd 1980

Church and Nation in a Secular Age, Darton Longman & Todd 1983

PAMPHLETS

A Biologist Looks at Life, SPCK 1965

A Scientific Look at Miracles, Church Lit. Assoc. Undated

CONTRIBUTIONS TO PUBLISHED BOOKS AND PAMPHLETS

'The uneasy truce between science and theology' in *Soundings: Essays concerning Christian Understanding*, edited by A. R. Vidler, Cambridge Univ. Press 1962

'Science and ethics', in *A Dictionary of Christian Ethics*, edited by John Macquarrie, SCM Press 1967

'A scientist looks at authority' in *The Bible Tells me so. Broadcast Talks on the Bible*, edited by Harold Loukes, SPCK 1967

'The meaning of marriage' in *Getting Married 1967*, British Med. Assoc. 1967

'The theology of creation' in *Christianity and Change*, edited by Norman Autton, SPCK 1971
'What is preaching?'
'Father and Son'
'Echoes'
'Faces'
'All Saints' in *Queen's Sermons*, edited by Trevor Rowe, Epworth Press 1973
'The Christian viewpoint' in *Church and Industry – a continuing debate*, Sheffield Ind. Mission 1977
'Christianity' in *A Dictionary of Medical Ethics*, edited by A. S. Duncan, G. R. Dunstan and R. B. Welbourn, Darton Longman & Todd 1977
'Can science survive?' in *Queen's Essays*, edited by J. Munsey Turner, The Queen's College, Birmingham 1980
'The biological manipulation of human life' in *Faith and Science in an Unjust World*, Part II, World Council of Churches 1980
'Theological reflections on compromise' in *Explorations in Ethics and International Relations: Essays in honour of Sydney D. Bailey*, Croom Helm 1981
'Creation'
'Evolution'
'God of the gaps'
'Model'
'Paradigm'
'Science and religion' in *A New Dictionary of Christian Theology*, edited by Alan Richardson and John Bowden, SCM Press 1983
'Marriage discipline' in *Rome '83: Returning the Pope's Visit*, BCC and Cath. Inf. Services 1983
'Discovering God in action' in *In Search of Christianity*, edited by Tony Moss, Firethorn Press 1986
'Brainwashing'
'Indoctrination'
'Science and ethics' in *Dictionary of Christian Ethics* (2nd edition) edited by John Macquarrie and James Childress, SCM Press 1986
'The house of laity' in *The Centenary of Lay Participation*, General Synod 1986

REPORTS BY AN INTER-DISCIPLINARY WORKING GROUP ON CURRENT MEDICAL/ETHICAL PROBLEMS UNDER THE AUSPICES OF THE NORTHERN REGIONAL HEALTH AUTHORITY. JOHN HABGOOD WAS CHAIRMAN AND MANY PUBLISHED REPORTS ARE OF HIS AUTHORSHIP

Ethics of selective treatment of spina bifida, *The Lancet* 11 January 1975

Prolongation of life in the deformed newborn, *The Journal of the North East England Faculty* (The Royal College of General Practitioners) September 1975

Ethical problems of repetitive research, *Journal of Medical Ethics* March 1977

Applications for ethical approval, *The Lancet* 14 January 1978

Ethical problems of screening for neural tube defects, *The Lancet* 15 July 1978

Sterilisation of the mentally handicapped, *The Lancet* 29 September 1979

The relationship between the medical profession and the media, Unpublished

The principles which should guide the ethical committees of area health authorities, Unpublished

The ethics of resource allocation, *Journal of Medical Ethics* March 1983

Confidentiality, *The Lancet* 13 August 1983

REPORTS OF COMMISSIONS, WORKING PARTIES AND STUDY GROUPS OF WHICH JOHN HABGOOD WAS CHAIRMAN OR MEMBER

Differentials, a report by the Central Stipends Authority CIO 1977

The sensitive scientist, British Association Study Group 1978

Deciding about energy policy, Council for Science and Society 1979

Towards visible unity: proposals for a covenant, the report of the Churches' Council for Covenanting, Churches' Council for Covenanting 1980

Alternative Service Book 1980 (John Habgood was Chairman of the Publication Committee and author of the Preface)

Towards understanding the Arab–Israeli conflict, the report of the British Council of Churches' visit to the Middle East, BCC 1981

Before it's too late. The challenge of disarmament, a complete record of the public hearing on nuclear weapons and disarmament organized by the World Council of Churches (John Habgood was Moderator), WCC 1983

One in prayer, addresses, sermons and comment from Christian

Church leaders at Canterbury, BCC and Catholic Truth Society 1984
Soviet pilgrimage, report of the British Council of Churches visit to USSR, BCC 1986
Changing Britain: social diversity and moral unity (John Habgood was Chairman of the working party), title not finalized, CIO 1987

SELECTED ARTICLES AND ESSAYS IN PERIODICALS (CHRONOLOGICAL ORDER)

'The electrical activity of the brain', *Science and Religion* Autumn 1949
'Sensitization of sensory receptors in the frog's skin', *Journal of Physiology* Nos. 1 and 2 1950
'Brains', *The Pilgrim News Letter* April 1950
'Physiology for the medical student', *Cambridge University Medical Society Magazine* 1950
'The scientific attitude', *The Pilgrim News Letter* July 1950
'Aunt Sally', *The Pilgrim News Letter* September 1950
'Static or dynamic?', *The Pilgrim News Letter*, December 1950
'On the virtuous life', *The Pilgrim News Letter* June 1951
'Personality', *The Pilgrim News Letter* October 1951
'Rewards', *Inter-Varsity* Autumn 1952
'Antidromic impulses in the dorsal roots', *Journal of Physiology* No. 2 1953
'Sermons good and bad', *Spectator* 1953
'Personality', *Homes and Parents* April 1953
'How to be good', *SCM Broadsheet* July 1957
'The attractiveness of science', *Theology* December 1958
'Scientific best-seller', *Cambridge Review* February 1960
'University sermon', *Cambridge Review* March 1960
'Ethics in the Church today', *Church Quarterly Review* October 1963
'Slow fuse', *Crucible* September 1965
'Moral discovery', *Theology* June 1966
'Guilt and forgiveness', *Theology* September 1966
'Censorship', *Theology* November 1966
'Biology and personality', *Frontier* November 1966
'They changed our thinking: Darwin and after', *Expository Times* January 1973
'Euthanasia: a Christian view', *Royal Society of Health Journal* June 1974
'Does God throw dice?', *Frontier* Autumn 1975

'Attitudes towards the sexually transmitted diseases', *Crucible* October 1975
'Directions for the Church of England', *Theology* May 1976
'Contraceptives for children', *Crucible* January 1977
'Experimentation on human beings', *The Franciscan* January 1977
'Technology and politics', *Crucible* January 1978
'Truth and Dr Steiner', *Listener* 11 May 1978
'On being a liturgical reviser', *Theology* March 1979
'Pros and cons of liturgical revision', *Times Higher Educational Supplement* 14 December 1979
'Technology and work', *CMS Magazine* July/September 1980
'Be like God', *Crucible* October–December 1979
'This deathblow to church unity', *The Times* 12 February 1982
'Evolution and the doctrine of creation' and 'Problems in medical ethics' (Public Lectures), *Insight* (Wycliffe College, Toronto) November 1982
'Protest and Protestants', *Times Higher Education Supplement* December 1983
'Difficulties with dogma' (Science and Religion), *The Times* 22 September 1984
'When symbols are keys to meaning', *The Times* 6 October 1984
'Medical ethics – a Christian view', *Journal of Medical Ethics* March 1985
'A circular argument that misses the point', *Guardian* April 1986
'A doctrinal role for the laity', *Church Times* 2 January 1987
'By wayward values to new vulnerabilities' (on the religious symbolism of AIDS), *The Times* 13 February 1987

Index